A VISIT TO THE VATICAN'S GREGORIAN MUSEUM

*FROM DIVINE AFRICAN SPIRITUALITY
TO CHRISTIAN THEOLOGY*

DR. DANIEL LAROCHE, MD

SMSW SWNW IRY IMHOTEP TEHUTI IMN-RA

Dedication

Africa is the origins of civilization, introducing spirituality, science and so much more to humanity.

I dedicate this book to the world, to all those who may not have a chance to travel to the Vatican to see the African artifacts from the Nile Valley.

Preface

I want to thank my parents, wife, children, friends, and family for their unconditional support and love.

In an imperfect world, I go by the name 'Daniel Laroche'. 'Daniel' is the biblical name my beloved parents gave to me, and 'Laroche' is the surname of my beloved father, who was from Jacmel, Haiti. Haiti was historically a colony of France, so I consider this a colonial name. Having genetic family heritage in Africa, specifically in Benin, Nigeria, Ghana, Congo, and Angola, in part inspired my African name, 'Smsw Swnw Iry Imhotep Tehuti Imn-Ra'. Some of my most significant events influenced the etymology of my African name. As a healer, I chose 'Smsw Swnw,' meaning 'Chief Doctor'. 'Iry' was one of the first ophthalmologists in the world, which also corresponds with my profession as an eye physician and surgeon. 'Imhotep' is the first recorded doctor. The name 'Tehuti' symbolizes thought, writing, scholarship, and authorship, while 'Imn-Ra' represents the unseen, which are parts of me that may be unknown to others now and in the future. In its fullness, my African name connotes an emotional break with my colonial name and a reconnection with African heritage.

During my visit to the Vatican, I learned of the Gregorian Museum, a comprehensive depository dedicated to the historical legacy of the Ancient Nile Valley. I was astonished that the ancient teachings and traditions of the Nile Valley were so revered by the Vatican, and eventually were altered into modern-day religions. It reinforced my prior knowledge of the greatness of the African Nile Valley civilizations, which had lasted for thousands of years. Their contributions still stand as a representation of their remarkable talents. At the museum, I took many pictures. Thus, working on this book not only included researching and photographing the artifacts but also involved field investigation and further examining the sources of the artifacts.

Symbolism in the teachings of the African Nile Valley holds profound importance as it serves as a bridge connecting humans to nature and the universe, embodying deep spiritual and cosmological meanings. Symbols in African traditional religion are not mere signs but carry rich logical layers that convey divine presence and mediate the relationship between the physical and metaphysical realms. The Nile River itself is a powerful symbol of life's cyclical nature—representing birth, death, and rebirth—and acts as a temporal and spiritual link between ancestors, present generations, and future descendants. This symbolism reflects a holistic African worldview, where all existence is interconnected through a shared spiritual energy that transcends time and space, fostering harmony between humans, nature, and the cosmos. Thus, symbolism in the Nile Valley teachings is essential for understanding the universe's rhythm, honoring ancestral wisdom, and maintaining cosmic harmony through an intimate relationship with nature.

Countless hours studying Ancient African traditions have made me a lifelong student. These great teachings inspire peace, excellence, scientific discovery, and immortality through writing. My motivation in writing this book is to impart information to those who may not receive the opportunity to visit the museum or study the epic impact of the Nile Valley on humanity and the exploitive practices others used to birth modern-day religion. I wrote this book with accompanying images to document, bear witness, and share this information with the world. I know many people will not have the opportunity to travel to the Vatican to see the artifacts and the current symbols along with the imagery of the Gregorian Museum. I wrote it to share what I saw during my walk through the museum in the order of my trip. I encourage all people to study and learn the African origins of civilization, for it is the genesis of antiquity.

TABLE OF CONTENTS

CHAPTER ONE

THE VATICAN, ITALY, AND THE TEHKEN

The Vatican is its own country within a country of Italy. The Vatican is recognized as a country due to its unique status as an independent city-state. It gained recognition as a country through the signing of the Lateran Treaty in 1929, which granted Vatican City the status of a sovereign state. This treaty resolved the political and religious turmoil in Italy at the time and established the Vatican as a separate entity with its own government and territory. Furthermore, the Vatican is a major historical epicenter of religious worship `and maintains a sizable collection of Ancient African artifacts. Seeing the presence of African history in the most unexpected place is amazing.

Italy has many Obelisks, and there are over 13 in Rome. The African name for Obelisk is Tehkenu. Many of the Tehkenus seen in Italy originated in Africa from the Nile Valley. A Tehkenu or Tehken is a tall four-sided, pointed pillar that tapers inward from its base towards its top, which is usually a pyramid shaped.

Every visitor embarks on a visual pilgrimage guided by the treasures and tales within the museum.

Photo credit courtesy of Gorringe, Henry
Honychurch (1885) Egyptian Obelisks, Nineteenth Century Collections Online (NCCO): Photography: The World through the Lens, John C. Nimmo.

The Gregorian Museum is an African jewel, tucked within the Vatican. In the museum, the pages of time turn gently beneath the gaze of ageless artifacts and scriptures, inviting us to witness its sacred corridors and hidden chambers. We can discover a repository of African wisdom and artistic brilliance, curated with precision and commitment to cultural preservation. This is where every exhibit and, every relic becomes a vessel, transporting us through the annals of the prior. This is where the past intertwines with the present. Every visitor embarks on a visual pilgrimage guided by the treasures and tales within the museum.

My adventure became an exploration of African artifacts removed from Kemet (now known as Egypt) and brought to Europe by the Vatican". Around the 1820s, the Vatican started collecting information and priceless items from the Nile Valley. Some churches at that time supported the establishment of colonial regimes. Many documented events in history explain how these artifacts made their way to Europe.

We know that the Vatican Museum was founded in 1506. Today, it has approximately 70,000 artifacts with over 20,000 on display_[1] and countless secrets lurking within its walls. The Gregorian Egyptian Museum at the Vatican is a series of nine rooms in the Belvedere Palace with one of the most fascinating galleries in the world. This collection was originally featured in a 16th-century, retreat apartment of Pope Pius IV. It was founded by Pope Gregory XVI, who was ruling the city at a time of great excitement about African Nile Valley history, following the first decipherment of hieroglyphics. A passion for learning initially drove Pope Gregory XVI, so he ordered that all African Nile Valley (Egyptian and "Egyptianized")

---

https://www.museivaticani.va/content/museivaticani/en/collezioni/musei/museo-gregoriano-egizio/museo-gregoriano-egizio.html.

artifacts in the pontifical states be gathered in a new museum. However, the real expert behind the establishment of the museum was Barnabite Father Giuseppe, who was assigned as its first curator. Barnabite Father Giuseppe himself was an eminent Egyptologist and disciple of Ippolito Rossellini, the known father of Egyptology in Italy.

In the 1750s, King Emanuel III instructed and funded the expedition of the famed Italian botanist Vitaliano Donati to Egypt, from where he brought back 300 artifacts from the Karnak temple complex_2. However, it is mainly believed that the conquest of Egypt and the incorporation into the Roman Empire created a new culture with the practices of Ancient Egypt. The Ancient Nile Valley-style architecture and sculpture (Tehkenus or Obelisks) were installed in the Roman fora at that time. This is how Auset, the African Egyptian mother Netert (goddess also renamed Isis by the Romans), had an immense impact throughout the Empire. Plus, Rome had already begun to receive an influx of Nile Valley culture around 58 BCE during the divisive period of the civil war. Much of this conflict was sourced through an intense rivalry between the Octavian in Rome and Mark Antony along with Cleopatra VII in Egypt.

During my trip, I was pleasantly surprised finding out that the Gregorian Museum houses a huge collection of African Nile Valley artifacts that I documented in many pictures, included in this book. Having discovered this unrecognized marvel, I really want to share this experience with the world for those who may not be able to see these precious artifacts. So, embark on a literary voyage with me—a journey that transcends borders and epochs, a journey into the heart

---

https://www.museivaticani.va/content/museivaticani/en/collezioni/musei/museo-gregoriano-egizio/sala-ii--costumi-funerari-dellantico-egitto.html.

4

of the Gregorian Museum, where the echoes of the past resonate, and the pages of history unfold in the presence of timeless artifacts. My book unveils a narrative that exceeds historical boundaries and connects us to the enduring spirit of human creativity, intellect, and reverence from an African origin.

"Seeing the presence of African history in the most unexpected place is amazing."

Photo by Daniel Laroche, MD

CHAPTER TWO
THE FALSE DOOR

My journey to the Gregorian Museum began with studying the Medu Neter (hieroglyphs) until one exquisite relic caught my eye: the False Door of Iry, one of the most revered Nile Valley artifacts.

This False Door stele belonged to Iri-en-achti, also known as Iry, a priest of Pharaoh Khufu in the Fourth Dynasty.

⌢ 𓄿 ⌣ 𓄿 Khufu

Iry's name is memorialized at the Great Pyramid of Giza, which is considered the most majestic edifice ever built.

𓇋 ⌣ 𓇋 Iry

As a fascinating archaeological and historical relic, the False Door of Iry provides a glimpse into the life and role of

Iry, the High Priest of Khufu [3]. Historically, Iry oversaw the construction and rituals of the tomb of Pharaoh Khufu, housed within the Great Pyramid of Giza. He held the esteemed position of High Priest during the reign of Pharaoh Khufu, who was recognized as one of Egypt's most iconic rulers of the Fourth Dynasty. Iry was a key administrative and ceremonial overseer, responsible for conducting rituals and ceremonies and managing the spiritual affairs surrounding the king. He was also known to be one of the first eye doctors.

Despite the term "false," these doors were not meant for physical passage but rather served as symbolic gateways between the worlds of the living and the dead. In the case of Iry, his False Door was a pathway for spiritual connection. It is meant to allow the living to communicate with their 'ka' (spirit) and offer them sustenance in the afterlife.

The door is intricately carved and decorated. Such doors were usually placed in mastabas (tombs) of ancient Egyptians [4]. It is sculpted with meticulous details, featuring inscriptions and scenes of rituals, offerings, and hieroglyphic texts that symbolize prayers and blessings. The artwork often portrayed Iry in his traditional regalia while he was engaged in sacred ceremonies. The design usually emphasized his role as a bridge between the earthly and divine realms.

---

https://www.museivaticani.va/content/museivaticani/en/collezioni/musei/museo-gregoriano-egizio/sala-i--reperti-epigrafici/stele-a-falsa-porta-di-iri.html.

Scholtz, S., Becker, M., MacMorris, L., and Langenbucher, A. 2023. "Iry" Egypt 2400 BCE: Iry, The First Known Ophthalmologist. Curiosities in Medicine. Springer, Cham. https://doi.org/10.1007/978-3-031-14002-0_41.

https://www.thearchaeologist.org/blog/the-false-doors-of-the-egyptian-tombs-a-threshold-between-the-worlds-of-the-living-and-the-dead.

The significance of the False Door of Iry is not only conveyed as a physical monument but also it is a conduit for perpetuating his spiritual legacy. Through the rituals conducted at the False Door, offerings and writings were held to ensure the eternal well-being of Iry's ka, such that a favorable existence is secured for him in the afterlife.

Understanding False Doors in Ancient African Nile Valley Traditions

The concept of false doors is a fascinating and distinctive feature in the funerary architecture of Ancient African Nile Valley. They are one of the architectural elements showcasing a unique symbolism in the traditions and spiritual beliefs of the ancient African Egyptians. These structures have been commonly incorporated into tombs and mortuary structures.

From a spiritual standpoint, the false door served as a symbolic portal between the worlds of the living and the dead. The ancient people of the Nile Valley believed that their deceased could travel between the realms of the living and the dead, and the false door facilitated that spiritual journey. Even in the tomb's designs, it was an essential component, representing a connection point through which the ka of the deceased could receive offerings and prayers from the living. The belief was quite important in ensuring a continuous and positive existence in the afterlife.

Architectural design

False doors were designed to resemble actual doors. The structure usually comprised of lintels, doorposts, and sometimes even knobs. It is merely a mimicry aimed to create a visual representation of a real-life entrance that the deceased could use to travel between the worlds. Adorned with inscriptions and intricate scenes, false doors depict the deceased involved in various activities such as receiving offerings, participating in rituals, or interacting with deities. These depictions were meant to invoke the favor of the Neteru

(Creator or God) and ensure that the dead is taken care of in the afterlife.

Societal Perspective

While false doors were present in the tombs of various social classes, they were especially found in the burials of the elite and the pharaohs. The complexity and grandeur of their structure often reflected the status and importance of the deceased. In some instances, they were incorporated into separate structures called 'offering chapels. These chapels were dedicated only to the family members and priests, so that they could conduct rituals and make offerings.

Symbolism of the West

In the Ancient African teaches of MAAT, the West was symbolically associated with the land of the dead. Sunsets occurred in the West that marked the end of each day. As the sun dipped below the horizon, it was believed to journey through the underworld during the night. Then, before emerging in the East, it was believed to signify rebirth and renewal. Therefore, the West became closely linked with the journey to the afterlife.

False doors evidently were placed on the west wall of the funerary chapel or offering chamber, which could symbolize the doorway through which the deceased could pass into the afterlife. Rituals and ceremonies conducted in front of the false door on the west wall were integral to the deceased's journey to the afterlife. Family members and priests were known to make offerings and recite prayers, or they would perform symbolic acts to ensure the well-being and perpetual existence of the deceased in the divine realm.

Mastabas

False doors were commonly found in mastabas (tombs). They were flat-roofed structures that marked the burials of non-royal individuals. These tombs often had a chapel with a false door where rituals could take place.

Royal Tombs

In royal tombs, such as those of the Pharaohs in the Nile Valley, false doors were sometimes included as part of the overall funerary complex. The symbolism and rituals associated with these doors were adapted to suit the unique needs and beliefs of the ruling elite.

False Door of Ipyhersesenbef, Saqqara 6th Dynasty, 223-2150 BCE,
Photo by Daniel Laroche, MD

In summary, false doors of the Nile Valley were more than architectural elements. Ancient African Egyptians believed that they were thresholds between the world of the living and the dead, through which a deity or the spirit of the deceased could enter and exit. They were usually the focus of a tomb's offering chapel, where family members would make offerings for the deceased on a special offering slab, placed at the front door. Most false doors are found on the west wall of a funerary chapel or offering chamber because the people of the Ancient Nile Valley associated the west with the land of the dead. In many mastabas, both husband and wife were buried with their own false door.

Stellae of Hatshepsut and Thutmose III, 18th Dynasty,
Reign of Hatshepsut, 1460 BCE, Photo by Daniel Laroche, MD

CHAPTER THREE

STELLAE

Q ueen Hatshepsut, the royal wife of Pharaoh Thutmose II, ordered a sandstone stela to commemorate the African city of Waset (later known as West Thebes), located about 800 kilometers south of the Mediterranean. The stellae, also spelled stele or stella, depicts the Neter Amon-Ra, giving Queen Hatshepsut two globular jugs. In the portrayal, she wears a blue crown (khepresh) throughout the presentation. She is with her nephew Thutmose III, who is becoming pharaoh and wears the white crown of Upper Egypt.

Stela

A stela is a standing stone slab used in Ancient Nile Valley Africa for dedication, remembrance, and demarcation. It is a vital artifact of primordial history because it predates and serves as a template for Western tombstones. These prehistoric monuments, often with intricate carvings and inscriptions, played many functions in Ancient African civilizations.

Where the white and Blue Nile rivers meet in Khartoum, Sudan, stela were used to record important events, define boundaries, and honor important people. They were elaborately carved with religious ceremonies, offerings, or the accomplishments of the honoree. These standing stones were more than monuments; they embodied the culture, traditions, and social values of ancient societies. They could encompass pivotal mythological symbolism and real people.

Over time, cultural exchanges, discoveries, and encounters brought the idea of honoring people with a stone monument to the West. Civilizations were known to exchange products, ideas, and traditions. Using standing stones for memorialization, thus, was incorporated into Western funeral rituals.

Tombstones evolved from this African origin to Europe and the Americas. They, like their ancient counterparts, mark the last resting place and connect the living and the dead. To honor the deceased, they are etched with names, dates, and even exquisite artwork.

The evolution from the African stela to the Western gravestone illustrates the human need to remember people in a tactile and permanent way. These standing stones demonstrate a basic human need to establish markers that last and honor our ancestors. The Names of Nsut Bitys, Pharaohs" or include transitional words or sentences to go from the "stele" to "Nsut Bitys"

As written, the relationship between "stele" and "pharaohs. In the previous figure, the names of Hatshepsut and Thutmose are written on the stela in the oval shen (cartouche). Hatshepsut's name is inscribed in the Medu Neter as MAAT-Ka-Ra, and Thutmose's name is written as Mn-Kherper-Ra.

The Nsut Bity would have five names. In Ancient Egypt, a king's name represented their might and their divinity. By the Middle Kingdom, the royal titulary included five names: the Heru name, the Netbi name, the Golden Horus name, the Praenomen/Throne name, and the Nomen/Birth name.

Heru Name: Heru was the Neter of the sky, kingship, and order. He was often depicted in imagery as a man with the head of a falcon. The pharaoh's name signified the belief that he was the earthly incarnation of Heru. His Heru name is epitomized by a falcon sitting atop a serekh, a rectangle that represents the façade of the king's palace and contains the name of the pharaoh in the Medu Neter writing.

Nebti Name: The word 'Netbi' means 'two ladies. The ladies in question were the goddesses of Upper and Lower Kemet Upper, Nekhbet, is represented by a vulture, and the Neter of Lower Egypt, Wadjet, is represented by a cobra. The Nebti name of the pharaoh reinforced that the pharaoh was the ruler of both Upper and Lower parts of Egypt.

Golden Heru Name: This name was depicted with a falcon and considered the hieroglyph for gold. It is thought to embody the idea that, as Heru, the pharaoh would be eternal since gold was associated with eternity.

Throne Name: The pharaoh (Nust Bity) was given the praenomen, also known as the throne name, at his or her ascension to becoming the ruler. It was enclosed in an oval shen (cartouche), which represented the royal name of the monarch. It usually included the name 'Re' or 'Ra', who was the Deity or Neter of the underworld, sky and earth, possessing power over Divine order and the sun.

The throne name was accompanied by the title 'He of the Sedge and the Bee', which is thought to denote that the pharaoh (nst bity) reigned both Upper and Lower Egypt. Ascertained from the papyrus, sedge represented Upper Egypt and the bee represented Lower Egypt.

Birth name: Nomen

The nomen was the birth name of the king, the name by which we know a pharaoh or Nust Bity today. The birth name would remain within a family, like a modern-day surname, which is how successive generations of pharaohs bore the same nomen. For instance, eleven pharaohs bore

the birth name Rameses. When a new name was devised, it was carefully chosen to convey the importance of the pharaoh and his divine connections. Tutankhamun, for example, means 'the living image of 'Amun', who was the Neter of the sun and air.

A pharaoh could change his name to reinvent himself. The pharaoh Amenhotep IV changed his name to Akhenaton to show his devotion to the sun Aten. He spent his rule advocating that his people should worship Aten only, but after his death, Atenism was abandoned in favor of the usual many Neters.

The birth name was contained within the cartouche, along with the name of the throne. Before the name came the epithet 'Son [or Daughter] of Re'.

Hatshepsut and Thutmose III

Hatshepsut, the daughter of a monarch, a woman unlike others. She was one of the few female pharaohs in the history of ancient Egypt, which spans thousands of years. Unfortunately, she did not inherit her kingdom in the same way that a man would have. In Ancient Nile Valley, only sons were permitted to succeed their fathers. Hatshepsut was born around the year 1504 BC, and when her father, King Thutmose I, passed away without any sons, she married her half-brother Thutmose II, who was only three years old at the time, to assist him in fulfilling his role as pharaoh.

As one of the most influential pharaohs in the history of the African Nile Valley[5], Hatshepsut, gave her country a significant deal of riches and artistic talents. She was the sponsor of one of the most successful trading voyages in Ancient African Nile Valley, which imported gold, ebony, and incense from a location known as Punt. It was most likely situated in what is now the country of Eritrea in Africa. She ensured that her legacy would live on by erecting buildings that are still

---

https://www.history.com/topics/ancient-egypt/hatshepsut.

standing today. She added tehkens (obelisks), each nearly 200 feet tall, to the enormous temple complex at Karnak (Luxor, Egypt).

Hatshepsut names

Name Type	Egyptian Name	Meaning	Medu Neter Name
Horus Name	Kanakht Merymaat	Mighty Bull, Beloved of Maat	
Nebty Name	(Two Ladies)	Protector goddesses of Egypt	
Golden Horus	(varies)	Eternal kingship	
Prenomen (Throne)	Maatkare	Truth is the soul of Re	
Nomen (Birth)	Hatshepsut	Foremost of Noble Ladies	

After her husband's death, Thutmose II, Queen Hatshepsut, became co-regent with her baby nephew-stepson, Thutmose III. Queen Hatshepsut became pharaoh and ruled alone for 22 years. Following her death, however, her name and likeness were removed from pharaoh monuments and inscriptions, destructing portrayals of her. Her successors even attempted large-scale rewritings of her contributions to history, possibly because she was a female pharaoh. *'Damnatio memoriae'* is the Latin term for this type of misuse of power.

In 1819, the Vatican bought a stela from her "co-regency" that provided information when Hatshepsut and Thutmose III shared authority. Hatshepsut and Thutmose III shaped Ancient Egypt's spiritual traditions and politics throughout the New Kingdom. Many inventive portrayals show both monarchs sacrificing Amun. This image confirms how religious devotion and political power are intertwined.

Hatshepsut is often shown making offerings to several deities, including Amun. The monumental Temple of Hatshepsut (*djeser-djeseru*) at Deir el-Bahari burial shrine is one of many works about her. There are scenes that show Hatshepsut wearing traditional African royal regalia and offering food, incense, and symbolic items. These depictions show her spiritual traditions and her political strategy of linking herself to the divine in legitimizing her power.

In the stride of Hatshepsut, Thutmose III made himself one of Egypt's most successful military leaders. Thutmose III, like his grandfather, often surrendered offerings to Amun and other deities. Thutmose III was a brilliant military commander with dual duties. These sequences highlight his political and spiritual roles. Thutmose III's military conquests expanded the Nile Valley Empire, while his devotion to spiritual traditions emphasized the importance of maintaining a healthy relationship with the Neteru (Gods).

As co-rulers, their contributions were part of Ancient Nile Valley spiritual traditions and ceremonies. The pharaohs showed their devotion to the Neteru and sent political signals to the people. Hatshepsut and Thutmose III strengthened their authority and legitimized their rule by stressing their divine connection.

These artistic depictions, carved on temple walls and preserved in inscriptions, reveal the complex interplay between traditions and politics in Ancient Kemet. Hatshepsut and Thutmose III left a visual legacy behind through their sacrifices to Amun, displaying the importance of spiritual traditions in their lives. Thus, the intricate weaving of spiritual and political life in Ancient Egyptian culture is a testament to its complexity.

When Hatshepsut made her physical transition in 1458 BC, the Nile Valley would not see another female monarch who was as powerful as she until Cleopatra ascended to the throne, another 1,400 years later.

In ancient Kemet (Egypt), the Stela of Nebsu had a prominent Eye of Heru, in which the Eye of Heru and the Eye of Ra possess similar attributes. The all-knowing eye remains an important symbol, signifying healing, protection, and well-being. It, also, suggests the senses of sight, sensation, taste, touch speech and thought along with the ability to manifest dreams and aspirations. The Eye of Heru, therefore, was elevated to the funerary offerings and temple rituals to the Neteru.

Stela of an official during the Armana period receiving many offerings, Photo by Daniel Laroche, MD

Stela of Nebsu, the overseer of the King's aviaries in the Middle Kingdom (2040-1640 BCE), Photo by Daniel Laroche, MD

A Royal Announcement

Stone scarab of Amenhotep III announcing his wedding to his soon to be wife Queen Tiye, Photo by Daniel Laroche, MD

Shen of Akenaton, Akhenaton-Amenohotep IV (1353–36 BCE), Photo by Daniel Laroche, MD

Nsut Bity (Pharaoh) Amenhotep IV introduced sweeping changes in the spheres of spirituality, architecture, and art (Amarna style). Near the main Neter of Amon at Karnak, he founded several new temples dedicated to Re-Harakhte, who was now provided with a lengthy epithet placed in two royal shens (cartouches) and was described as "the light which is in the sun's disk (Aton). The Neter Aton was no longer portrayed in anthropomorphic form or similar to a human but as the sun's disk itself, elevated to the heavens and extending its multiple rays down over the royal family. Each ray ended in a tiny hand with which the Aton might offer the sign of life to the king and queen or even embrace their limbs and crowns"[9].

Ankhs signifying life being poured over Pharaoh Amenhotep III Menkeprera, Throne name for Tuthmose,
Photo by Daniel Laroche, MD

Dorman, Peter F.. "Akhenaten". *Encyclopedia Britannica*, 18 Aug. 2023, https://www.britannica.com/biography/Akhenaten. Retrieved 12.27.2023.

Scribed in the African Pyramid Text, the oldest written language of humans, the Stela on page 29 depicts the performance of various purification rituals, which predated Christian baptism.

Utterance 93 of the Pyramid Text:

"Wash yourself, Unas, open your mouth with the Eye of Heru!

Call your Ka, like Ausar, that he may protect you against every kind of wrath of the dead!

Unas, receive this, your bread which is the Eye of Heru!"[10]

A Stela of an offering being made to Ausar,
Photo by Daniel Laroche, MD

From Pyramid Texts Spell 527, Commentary".
Context of Scripture Online. Retrieved 2023-03-14.

In the stela depicting an offering made to Ausar, he is often shown wearing the Atef Crown. The Atef Crown is a combination of Upper Kemet's white crown, the Hedjet, and ostrich feathers on either side. It also often includes a golden disk at its tip. The ostrich feathers, similar to those representing Ma'at, exemplify truth, justice, morality, and balance.

A Stela of Neferrenpet making an offering to the Neter Ptah.
Memphis, 20ᵗʰ Dynasty (1196-1070 B.C.)
Photo by Daniel Laroche, MD

Conceived in the Nile Valley traditions, the Neter Ptah birthed the entire world and brought it into existence through the authority of imaginative speech. Dating back to the Twenty-second Dynasty of Egypt, a Ptah mantra declares, "crafted the world in the design of his heart." The Shabaka Stone from the Twenty-fifth Dynasty states that Ptah "gave life to all the Neters [Gods] and their kas [souls] as well through this heart and this tongue." In the great Ptah epithets, his significance in the societal traditions of the Ancient Nile Valley unfolds:

- *Ptah the begetter of the first beginning*

- *Ptah lord of truth*

- *Ptah lord of eternity*

- *Ptah who listens to prayers*

- *Ptah master of ceremonies*

- *Ptah master of justice*

- *Ptah the beautiful face*

Ptah is generally represented in the guise of a man with green skin, contained in a shroud sticking to the skin, wearing the divine beard and holding a scepter, which combine three powerful symbols of Ancient Nile Valley Tradition:

- The *Was* scepter

- The sign of life, *Ankh*

- The *Djed* pillar[11]

These combined symbols indicate the three creative powers of the god: power (was), life (ankh) and stability (djed).

Allen, James P. *Genesis in Egypt: The Philosophy of Ancient Egyptian Creation Accounts*. New Haven, 1988.

A Stela dedicated to the Neter Khonsu
Thebes, Roman Period 1st BC to 1st AD
Photo by Daniel Laroche, MD

As the Nile Valley deity (Neter) of the Moon, Khonsu's name means traveler. He often was viewed as the nightly traveler of the moon in the sky. Similarly to Tehuti, Khonsu signaled the passing of time and was valuable to all new life. At Luxor, he was included in the "Theban Triad" with Amun as his father and Mut as his mother. On the top of the Stela is a winged sun disk. Heru-Behutet, winged sun disk, is the symbol of the divine principle that safeguards our existence from the injustices of others. It works sternly through the law that states, "you reap what you sow"; be consistent in being just with others, and one will be spiritually protected by this divine power. Nile Valley traditions were meant to pass generational knowledge and wisdom.

Khonsu name in Medu Neter

Khonsu

Ausar, the Neter of Fertility, Agriculture, the Afterlife, and the Deceased, Photo by Daniel Laroche, MD

CHAPTER FOUR

AUSAR (OSIRIS)

K nown to the Greeks as Osiris, the Ancient Neter Ausar, popularly described as 'the God' who oversaw the afterlife, underworld, and deceased. He is usually depicted with green skin and a beard, like the pharaoh, with two large ostrich feathers on his crown and legs, half draped like a sahu (mummy). Ausar was one of the first to be affiliated with detailed mummy wrapping. One of the stories recorded is when his brother, 'Set', cut him up into pieces after killing him. Ausar's, wife Auset, found all the pieces and enclosed them, enabling Ausar to return to life. Ausar is often seen in African Nile Valley traditions holding a flail and a symbolic crook.

A typical large writing of Ausar (Osiris) in Medu Neter is:

- ⸙\ (the throne symbol, Gardiner sign Q3) representing "ws" or "ꜣw"

- ⸗ (the folded cloth or "s" sound)

- ⸜ (the mouth, "r" sound)

While 'Osiris' is the Greek name, in Egyptian hieroglyphs Ausar appears in many forms—including Aser, Ausar, Asar, Asari, Ausir, Ausare, Usire, Usir, Wser, or Wesir, translated as 'Almighty' or 'The Powerful.' Many tributes and rituals revered him for thousands of years. He was also the symbol of authority as seen with the shepherd's crook which supports this identification, as recognized by many archaeologists[12].

The Story of Ausar

After Ausar's resurrection, Auset mythologically transformed into a kite and circled Ausar to attract his seed. This allowed Auset to conceive Heru, who was born in the Nile Delta and named after the river.

To become Lord of the underworld, afterlife, and death, Ausar traveled to the land of the dead. The whole African Nile Valley, thus, revered Ausar; they acknowledged him as the Neter of the underworld, afterlife, life, death, and regeneration.

It was believed that celebrating the tradition of Ausar and living in MAAT one had to live a good life to bring salvation after death. Some people worship Ausar still in this way. The story of Ausar ends with his son Heru, avenging his death, defeating his uncle Set, and becoming King of the Living[13].

Ancient Africans of the Nile Valley prioritized Ausar meditation in their daily lives. The death of Ausar at the hands of Set and his 72 accomplices was recalled annually during worship. They devoted themselves to achieve the moral compass of MAAT.

---

https://www.ancient-egypt-online.com/osiris.html.

https://www.twinkl.com.pk/teaching-wiki/ancient-egyptian-god-of-the-dead-osiris.

{MAAT}

Maat is the ancient African Nile Valley concept of truth, balance, order, harmony, law, morality, and justice. The Netert (goddess) is the mystical manifestation of this ethos, embodying its virtues in divine form. She represents the ethical and moral principles that governed both the cosmos and human society, ensuring that the universe remained in a state of proper order rather than chaos.

Maat was often depicted as a woman with an ostrich feather on her head, which symbolized truth and justice. She was considered the daughter of the sun god Ra and closely associated with Tehuti (Thoth), the god of wisdom.

Maat's principles were fundamental to ancient African Nile Valley life and governance; pharaohs upheld Maat to legitimize their rule and maintain cosmic and social order.
In the afterlife, Maat's feather was used in the
"Weighing of the Heart" ceremony to judge the souls of the deceased, determining if they were worthy of eternal life.

As a result, they held several rites to celebrate his name, activities, and traits in preparation to see him in the afterlife.

Symbolizing Kemet's first king, the insignia of Ausar—the flail and shepherd's staff—became important to sentinet king successors. The representation of Ausar was regarded as ideal, thus later African Nile Valley Pharoahs tried to emulate his essence. The followers of Ausar believed he brought peace and unity.[14] They adored Ausar and believed that honoring him would benefit the African Nile Valley people. They celebrated him for eternal fertility, prosperity, and agricultural riches for thousands of year

CHAPTER FIVE

OFFERING TABLES

I n the Ancient African Nile Valley, offering tables were among the most important, ritual items that served only burial ceremonies. Food offerings to the deceased were placed on plant mats in early Pharaonic times. Then, Old Kingdom-style stone tables replaced the plant mats. Over time, several meals and drinks were added. Stelas on burial site walls depict offering tables. Both sites have historical significance for the respect of the deceased.

The tables were shaped like the hieroglyph "Hotep," meaning *"to be satisfied, at peace"*. The tables also have a passage for liquids to flow over them. Stone-crafted offering tables provided a place for gifts to symbolically nourish the dead.

Hotep in Medu Neter

Offering tables were often inscribed with religious invocations and images of Auset (the wife of Ausar) or other deities such as Anubis. Items placed on the tables included bread, geese, pigeons, beer, wine, water, oxen, and even non-food offerings such as linen, alabaster, and ointments. If certain items could not be physically provided, they were represented in Medu Neter/ hieroglyphic text on the table. A "banner," a detailed list of donations, sometimes followed the inscription[6]

---

https://historicaleve.com/offering-tables-in-ancient-egypt/.

CHAPTER SIX
QUEENS, NETERS, AND NETERTS

Image of Mummy of Amenirdis, 25th Dynasty, Kushitic Princess Photo by Daniel Laroche, MD

Amenirdis I, whose throne name was Hatneferumut, was the Queen wife of Amun during the 25th Dynasty of the Nile Valley Kingdom. She was born in the Kingdom of Kush, the daughter of Pharaoh Kashta and Queen Pebatima, and was later adopted by Shepenupet I. As shown in several artifacts from the period, she went on to rule as a high priestess, approximately between 714 and 700 BCE under the reigns of Shabaka and Shabataka.

Her mummy is displayed at the Vatican. In the Ancient African Nile Valley, this would have been unacceptable, as her remains were meant to rest undisturbed so that her soul could be at peace with the ancestors. The exposed body reveals her deeply melanated African skin.

Medu Neter spelling for Amenirdis I (feminine):

A along with Shepenupet I, she is depicted in the Ausar-Hekadjet temple within the Karnak temple complex and in Wadi Gasus. She is mentioned on two offering tables, five statues, a stela, and several small objects, including scarabs. The Nubian Museum in Aswan, Upper Kemet holds a statue of Amenirdis I that is carved from granitoid and decorated in gold leaf. The statue itself shows her decorated in the Egyptian style with similar portrayals to the deities, Auset and Hathor.

The turquois-colored beads on her sahu (mummy) connect her to the Neter Hathor following a tradition that preceded her by over a thousand years. She has several silver and gold amulets, including her heart scarab, which symbolically weighs her heart against a feather in the afterlife. Upon her death, she was buried in a tomb on the grounds of Medinet Habu.

Queen Tuya

Queen Tuya, 19th Dynasty, reign of Rameses II (1290-1224 BC), The statue was taken from Luxor by Caligula.

Photo by Daniel Laroche, MD and Luxor by Caligul

Queen Tuya: Mother of Pharaohs and Pillar of the Nineteenth Dynasty

Queen Tuya (also known as Tuy or Muat-Tuya) was a prominent royal woman of the Nineteenth Dynasty in the Ancient African Nile Valley. As the wife of Pharaoh Seti I and the mother of the legendary Ramesses II—often called "Ramesses the Great"—Tuya played a pivotal role in the royal court and the political landscape of the New Kingdom.

Noble Lineage and Family Connections

Tuya was the daughter of Raia, a distinguished military officer who held the title "Lieutenant of the Chariotry." This military background infused her lineage with prestige and influence. Her marriage to Seti I further solidified her status at court.

Tuya was the mother of:

- Ramesses II (her most famous son, who became one of Kemet's greatest pharaohs)
- Tia, her daughter, who married a high-ranking civil servant also named Tia
- Henutmire (possibly her daughter, though some sources suggest she may have been a granddaughter or a secondary wife of Ramesses II)

Role and Accomplishments

Influential Queen Consort

As queen consort to Seti I, Tuya was more than a royal wife but also an advisor and supporter in matters of state and traditions. Numerous monuments and inscriptions bear witness to her presence, reflecting her respected status.

Mother of the Pharaoh

Tuya's most enduring legacy is as the mother of Ramesses II, whose reign marked a golden age of ancient Kemet's power, monumental architecture, and cultural achievement. As "Mother of the King" (mwt-nsw), she held a position of immense honor and was often depicted alongside her son in statues and reliefs.

Political Influence

Tuya's influence extended beyond ceremonial duties. As Queen Mother, she likely played a key role in court politics, succession, and maintaining dynastic stability stability. Her wisdom and experience would have been invaluable during the transition from Seti I to Ramesses II.

Spiritual Patronage

Tuya participated in spiritual rituals and was associated with several temples. She is depicted in the Ramesseum (the mortuary temple of Ramesses II) and had her own statues and shrines, indicating her importance in state-sponsored spirituality.

Honored in Life and Death

Tuya lived to see her son's long and prosperous reign. She was buried in the Valley of the Queens (QV80), where the grandeur of her tomb reflects her elevated status. Her name and image appear in temples at Abydos, Luxor, and Thebes, ensuring her memory endures.

Legacy

Queen Tuya's life bridged two of Egypt's most illustrious rulers. Her wisdom, noble birth, and political acumen helped shape the royal family during a period of great prosperity and expansion. Today, she is remembered as a matriarch whose influence resonated throughout the Nile Valley and whose legacy is immortalized in stone.[16]

Grajetzki, Wolfram (2005) *Ancient Egyptian Queens: A Hieroglyphic Dictionary*, Golden House Publications.

Queen Arsinhoe II

Statue of Queen Arsinoe II, Ptolemaic period, Reign of Ptolemy II (285-264 BC), Photo by Daniel Laroche, MD

Arsinoë II was a Ptolemaic queen and co-regent of the Ptolemaic Kingdom of Ancient Egypt. She was given the Egyptian title 'King of Upper and Lower Egypt ', making her Pharaoh as well. Arsinoe was Queen of Thrace, Anatolia, and Macedonia through her marriage to King Lysimachus[17].

Beyond their own capacity, the lives and legacies of these queens were deeply shaped by the divine forces they revered. To fully understand the power and identity of these queens, it is essential to consider the deities who influenced their rule and roles.

Nebhet (Nephthys)

Nebhet was the daughter of the Neters Geb and Nut. She was associated with mourning, the night/darkness, temple services, childbirth, protection, magic, health, embalming, beer, and the dead. She was typically paired with her sister Netert Auset in funerary rites because of their role as protectors of the mummy and the Netert Ausar and as the sister-wife of Set.

In the Pyramid Texts, Nephthys emerges as the Highest One, a Netert of the Heliopolitan Ennead during the Fifth Dynasty. Nephthys is the sister of Auset and accomplice to the warrior deity. As the protector of the Highest One, she personifies the death experience, just as Auset embodies the birth experience. She is recognized in several Ancient African Nile Valley cosmologies and temple theologies as the "Helpful" or the "Excellent", which describes a Netert who exemplifies vigilant guardianship and divine cooperation.

Nephthys is also considered the mother of the funerary deity Anubis (Inpu). In Nubia, she is believed to be the wife of Anubis, who appears as the son of Bastet or Isis. Nephthys, on the contrary, is contemplated as the aunt of Heru but often appears as his mother. Sometimes, she is viewed as the wife of

---

Carney, Elizabeth Donnelly (2013). *Arsinoe of Egypt and Macedon: A Royal Life*. Oxford University Press. ISBN 978-0-19-971101-7.

Heru. As the primary wet nurse of "the incarnated, pharaonic deity Heru", Nephthys also was acknowledged as the caregiver of the reigning pharaoh himself. Although other deities could execute this role, Nephthys was mostly depicted as such in contrast to sometimes portrayed as a ruthless deadly force, which used her fiery breath to incinerate the pharaoh's enemies.

As described in the Pyramid Texts, the recently departed pharaoh navigated the different layers of the afterlife (Duat) with the assistance of Nephthys and sometimes Auset. As a critical force of heavenly transition, Nephthys empowered the pharaoh to become stronger for his journey. Later, the same divine power also applied to all the deceased. She was esteemed as an essential companion whom the evildoers feared her as similarly to Auset. This helped to enforce a strong moral compass in society.

Portrayed as a woman with outstretched falcon wings, symbolizing protection, Nephthys was associated with the piercing, mournful screech of the Egyptian hawk or kite. The wailing woman reminded Ancient Egyptians of the lamentations offered for the deceased. She was also identified with putrefaction and death, and often depicted as a crowned deity in the hieroglyphs. At the top of the enclosure, her name represented a combination of signs for the sacred temple encasing (ḥwt) and the symbol for mistress or lady (nb).

Nebhet and Auset, Photo by Daniel Laroche, MD

Nebhet name in Medu Neter

Auset (Isis)

Auset, the Netert of love, healing, fertility, magic, and the moon, was the most revered divinity in Ancient African Nile Valley. Even under Greek rule, she was accepted as 'Aset' or 'Eset'. Later, she appeared in Roman mythology, Known to the Greeks and Romans as Isis, Auset was later incorporated into Roman mythology. Because her worship remained widespread, historians have compared the Virgin Mary—a central figure in Christian theology—to Auset, noting that

Mary upholds similar roles as a divine mother, protector, and symbol of compassion[18].

In the Medu Neter (hieroglyphic), Auset was often represented as a beautiful woman in a sheath dress with a solar disk and cow's horns on her head as a sign of the throne. She was closely tied to the Ancient Nile Valley monarchy. She appeared as a scorpion, bird, pig, or cow throughout history.

However, Auset was not mentioned before the 5th Dynasty (2465–2325 BCE), but the Pyramid Texts, written between 2350 and 2100 BCE, mentioned her often and showed her supporting the deceased ruler. After concepts of the afterlife became more democratic, Auset was allowed to help all Nile Valley citizens who had died.

Auset name in Medu Neter

Stories of Auset, Ausar, and Set echo in various forms within modern religions, including parallels to the Virgin Mary's Immaculate Conception of Jesus.

---

https://www.thecollector.com/who-is-the-egyptian-goddess-isis-7-facts/.

Anpu (Anubis)

Photo by Daniel Laroche, MD

Anubis (also known as Inpu, Inpw, and Anpu) is the Ancient Nile Valley Neter of mummification, funerary rites, guardian of tombs, and guide to the afterlife as well as the patron Neter of lost souls and the helpless. He is one of the oldest Neters of the Nile Valley, most likely developed from the earlier jackal Neter Wepwawet, with whom he is often confused.

Anubis' image is seen on royal tombs from the First Dynasty during the Ancient Nile Valley (c. 3150-2890 BCE). Through oral tradition in the Predynastic Period, he was thought to have developed in response to wild dogs and speed hounds called Sebs, known for digging up newly buried corpses. In the Ancient Nile Valley from 6000 to 3150 BCE, the Kemetic people believed a powerful canine Neter was the best protection against wild canines destorying burial sites. However, no indigenous writings support this belief.

Photo by Daniel Laroche, MD

Anubis name in Medu Neter

Maahes

Maahes, Photo by Daniel Laroche, MD

In the sacred traditions of Ancient Nile Valley (Medu Neter), Maashes often was envisioned with a man's head and a lion's body, holding a sharp instrument and lotus flowers. The people of the Nile Valley believed the lion-headed Neter Maahes was the son of the creator Neter Ptah and the female Neter Sekhmet. He was a feared Neter whose sphere of influence included war, protection, and the weather. As a feline deity, the name Maahes means the capable one with the titles of *The Scarlet Lord*, *Lord of Slaughter*, and *Wielder of the Knife*. Identified with such words as *mashead*, *strength*, *power*, and *prince*, Maahes is a lion with powerful qualities in the Medu Neter and linked with the pharaohs as a noted supporter of Ancient Nile Valley.

He was considered the offspring of Ra, along with the catlike Netert Bastet or Sekhmet. Sometimes, branded with another child of Sekhmet, Nefertum, Maahes during the nightly voyages of Ra supposedly fought the viper Apep, the arch enemy of Ra. He was associated with Nefertum, who symbolized the lotus flowers[19].

Maahes in Medu Neter

Wilkinson, Richard H. (2003). *The Complete Gods and Goddesses of Ancient Egypt*. Thames & Hudson. pp. 178–179.

Serket

Netert Serket, Showed with the Head of a Woman
and the Body of a Scorpion
Photo by Daniel Laroche, MD

Serket is sometimes acknowledged as the offspring of Neith and Khnum, making Apep and Sobek her siblings. She did not seem to have any temples in her honor.

Illustrated as a scorpion, Serket has the torso of a reptile and the head of a woman. In Ancient Kemetic (Egyptian) traditions, Serket is the scorpion deification and the Netert of poisonous bites and stings. Her name means one who tightens the air paths because she paralyzes her victims. Her name, contrarily, can translate as the unrighteous sting that opens airways for breath.

She defended the Ancient people of the Nile Valley from the deadliest scorpion in North Africa, the death stalker (now known as Leiurus Quinquestriatus), whose bite killed upon contact. When the evil snake-demon Apep was captured, the deity Serket was thought to shield the people from him. Thus, she was viewed as a central Netert figure and sometimes considered the patron of the pharaohs. Her close association with the early monarchs suggests she protected them, particularly from rulers Scorpion I and Scorpion II.

In the Ancient African Nile Valley, venomous snake stings proved countless fatalities, and Serket became the watcher of the deceased. She was, therefore, considered the protector of the embalmers' work area and canopic jars that stored body parts, which was later deified as Heru's son, Qebehsenuef. As the defender of canopic jars, she gained a strong affiliation with Auset, Neith, and Nephthys, who also executed similar responsibilities. Eventually, she was identified most notably with Isis in which they shared similar parentage and imagery. Serket, finally, was relegated to a mere aspect of Isis, whose cult had become mainstreamed.

Serket name in Medu Neter

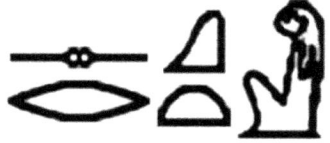

TEHUTI

Baboon Tehuti, Photo by Daniel Laroche, MD

Tehuti appeared as both an ibis, bird-headed man, and a baboon in Kemetic traditions. His personality remained consistent across these representations. However, while his baboon imagery predated his ibis-headed portrayals, the latter emerged as his primary depiction over time.[20]

Sages of all eras and civilizations proclaimed Tehuti as the most spiritual and intellectual master of all time. Thus, he was revered as the greatest master ever. The Ancient African sages declared Tehuti the one who was so old that he became a myth. They considered Tehuti as the one who delivered them the Medu Neter. **Medu Neter** (also spelled mdw ntr, medu netcher, or metu neter) is the **ancient African term for their system of writing**, commonly known today as hieroglyphics. The phrase literally translates to **"divine words," "language of the gods,"** or **"divine speech."** In this context:

- **"Medu"** means "words" or "speech."

- **"Neter"** (or "ntr") means "god," "divine," or "sacred."

Medu Neter was used to inscribe spiritual, historical, and administrative texts on temple walls, monuments, tombs, papyrus scrolls, and other artifacts from ancient Kemet (Egypt). It is considered the world's oldest known writing system and was believed by the ancient Africans of the Nile Valley to be a sacred language that conveyed the words and principles of the divine.

The writing system combined logographic, alphabetic, and phonetic symbols, and was central to the spiritual,

---

Budge, *The Gods of the Egyptians*, Vol. 1, p. 400.

cultural, and intellectual life of ancient Egypt. Medu Neter not only recorded historical events and daily affairs but also expressed the Egyptians' cosmology, spirituality, and worldview, symbolizing the connection between the human and the divine.

In the end, Tehuti was promoted to the status of a god-man. Then, he was elevated to the position of the Neter of knowledge, Neter of medicine, Neter of healing, and guardian of priest-physicians. He was also uplifted to the Neter of the scribes and the god of writing, communications, language, architecture, mathematics, accounting, physics, astronomy, and science.

According to Theodor Hopfner, his name written as *dhwty* originated from the word *dhw*, which is claimed as the oldest known name for the ibis and normally written as *hbj*. The addition of *ty* connotes that he possessed the attributes of the ibis bird.[1] Hence Tehuti's name suggests, "He who is like the ibis", based on this interpretation.

Using older transcriptions, other forms of *dhwty* include *Jehuti, Jehuty, Tahuti, Tehuti, Zehuti, Techu,* or *Tetu.* Tehuti—also known as Thoth—was referred to by multiple titles, similar to the pharaonic titulary. These include *A, Sheps, Lord of Khemennu, Asten, Khenti, Mehi, Hab, and A'an.*

In addition, Thoth was also known by specific aspects of himself. For instance, the Moon Neter I̲ah-Djehuty (*j3h-dhw.ty*) would represent the Moon for the entire month. The Greeks related Thoth to their god Hermes because of his similar attributes and functions. In Greek, one of Thoth's titles was τρισμέγιστος (*trismégistos), translating to denote,* "Thrice great", so Hermes was recognized as Trismegistus.

Tehuti's roles in African Nile Valley mythology were many. He was credited with the creation of the African Nile Valley hieroglyphs and the invention of writing, serving as the scribe of the Neters. In the underworld, Duat, he appeared as the ape Aani and the Neter of equilibrium with the responsibility of weighing the deceased's heart against the feather.[21].

Tehuti name in Medu Neter

Hieroglyphs verified, in part, in Budge, *The Gods of the Egyptians*, Vol. 1, p. 402, and Collier and Manley, p. 161.

Verner, Miroslav (2013). Temple of the World: Sanctuaries, Cults, and Mysteries of Ancient Egypt. American University in Cairo Press. p. 149. ISBN 978-977-416-563-4.

Budge, *The Gods of the Egyptians*, Vol. 1.

AMUN-RA

Amun Ra, Black Granite, 19th Dynasty Reign of Seti I
(1306 - 1290 BC), Photo by Daniel Laroche, MD

Amun (also Amon, Ammon, Amen, and Amun-Ra) is the Ancient Neter of the sun and air. He is one of the most important Neters of Ancient Nile Valley who rose to prominence at Luxor at the beginning of the period of the New Kingdom (1570-1069 BCE). His followers were the most powerful and popular in Egypt for centuries.

He is usually depicted as a bearded man wearing a headdress with a double plume or, after the New Kingdom, as a ram-headed man or simply a ram, symbolizing fertility in his role as Amun-Min. His name means 'the hidden one', 'invisible', and 'mysterious of form'. Unlike most other Egyptian gods, he was considered the Neter of All who encompassed every aspect of creation.

Amun is first mentioned in the Pyramid Texts (2400-2300 BCE) as a local Neter of Luxor along with his consort Amaunet[22].

Amun name in Medu Neter

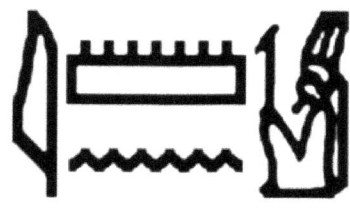

Stark, Rodney (2007). *Discovering God: The Origins of the Great Religions and the Evolution of Belief* (1st ed.). New York: HarperOne. p. 405. ISBN 978-0-06-117389-9.

BES

Bes, a Neter of the Nile Valley, represented as a dwarf with a large head, goggle eyes, protruding tongue, bowlegs, bushy tail, and usually a crown of feathers. The name 'Bes' is now used to designate a group of deities of similar appearance with a wide variety of ancient names. The Neter's figure was portrayed on mirrors, ointment vases, and other personal articles. He was associated with music and childbirth. He had representation in the birth houses and was devoted to the dwarf Neter.

People in Upper Egypt started venerating Bes long before people in Lower Egypt. The word "bes" means "cat" in Nubian, suggesting a possible Nubian or southern origin of Bes. Bes originally looked like a cat standing on his hind legs. After becoming more anthropomorphic, he usually was depicted with a leopard skin around his neck, resembling more like a dwarf.

Bes, Photo by Daniel Laroche, MD

Thirteen dwarf figurines were found at *Tell el-Farkha* (a predynatistic location), the largest group of such figurines so far discovered anywhere in Egypt. The images of dwarfs in art and their buried statuettes in the immediate vicinity of tombs of the kings and aristocracy indicate that dwarfs played an important role in the Ancient Nile Valley culture. The collection found a *Tell el-Farkha* attracted particular attention because of the high level of workmanship of most of them as well as the realistic facial expressions and the depiction of their bodies. They were far more skillfully crafted than any of the previously known earlier dwarf sculptures.

Bes name in Medu Neter

Carr, Karen (2017-06-18). "Who was the African god Bes?". Quatr.us Study Guides. Retrieved 2023-07-05.

SEKHMET

Sekhmet, The Powerful Neter of Ancient African Nile Valley Photo by Daniel Laroche, MD

Sekhmet, one of the most iconic deities of Ancient African Nile Valley, embodies duality and balance. Known as "The Powerful One," she is revered for her fierce nature as a warrior Netert and her nurturing role as a healer. Her lion-headed visage, often adorned with a sun disk and uraeus (a serpent symbol), reflects her connection to the sun Neter Ra and her role as the protector of the divine order.

Origins and Mythology

Sekhmet is closely associated with Ra, the sun Neter, as his daughter and the manifestation of his vengeful power, referred to as the "Eye of Ra." In mythology, she was sent by Ra to punish humanity for their disobedience. Her ferocity led to a bloody rampage that nearly annihilated humanity until Ra tricked her into drinking beer dyed red to resemble blood. This act pacified her, transforming her destructive energy into calmness and healing[23].

Sekhmet's dual nature is evident in her roles. While she could unleash plagues and destruction, she was also invoked to repel off disease and heal the sick. This paradox symbolizes the Ancient Africans of the Nile Valley understanding of life's delicate equilibrium between creation and destruction.

Iconography and Worship

Sekhmet is typically depicted as a lion-headed woman, emphasizing her strength and ferocity. Her statues, crafted with meticulous detail, are among the most numerous in Ancient African Nile Valley art. Over 700 statues were created during the reign of Amenhotep III alone, reflecting her immense significance. These statues were believed to pacify Sekhmet's wrath while invoking her protective and healing powers.

Her primary centers where she was celebrated were Memphis and Leontopolis, where she was worshipped alongside Ptah, her consort, and Nefertum, their son. Sekhmet's priests were renowned healers, further solidifying her association with medicine and protection against plagues.

Cultural Significance

Sekhmet's presence permeated the Ancient African Nile Valley traditions. Her statues served not only religious purposes but also political ones by legitimizing pharaohs' authority and maintaining societal cohesion. As a symbol of divine power and protection, she was deeply intertwined with the fabric of daily life.

Modern interpretations highlight Sekhmet's relevance beyond antiquity. She continues to inspire scholars, artists, and spiritual practitioners worldwide. Her principles resonate with themes of transformation, balance, and the interplay between destruction and renewal.

Legacy

Sekhmet remains one of Ancient African Nile Valley's most enduring figures. Her statues stand as testaments to artistic ingenuity and spiritual devotion. Through her duality—both fierce protector and compassionate healer—she offers profound insights into the beliefs about life's complexities of Ancient Africans of the Nile Valley.

Sekhmet embodies the power of transformation and balance. Her legacy as a warrior goddess and healer continues to captivate modern audiences, bridging the past with present understandings of strength, resilience, and renewal.

Sekhmet name in Medu Neter

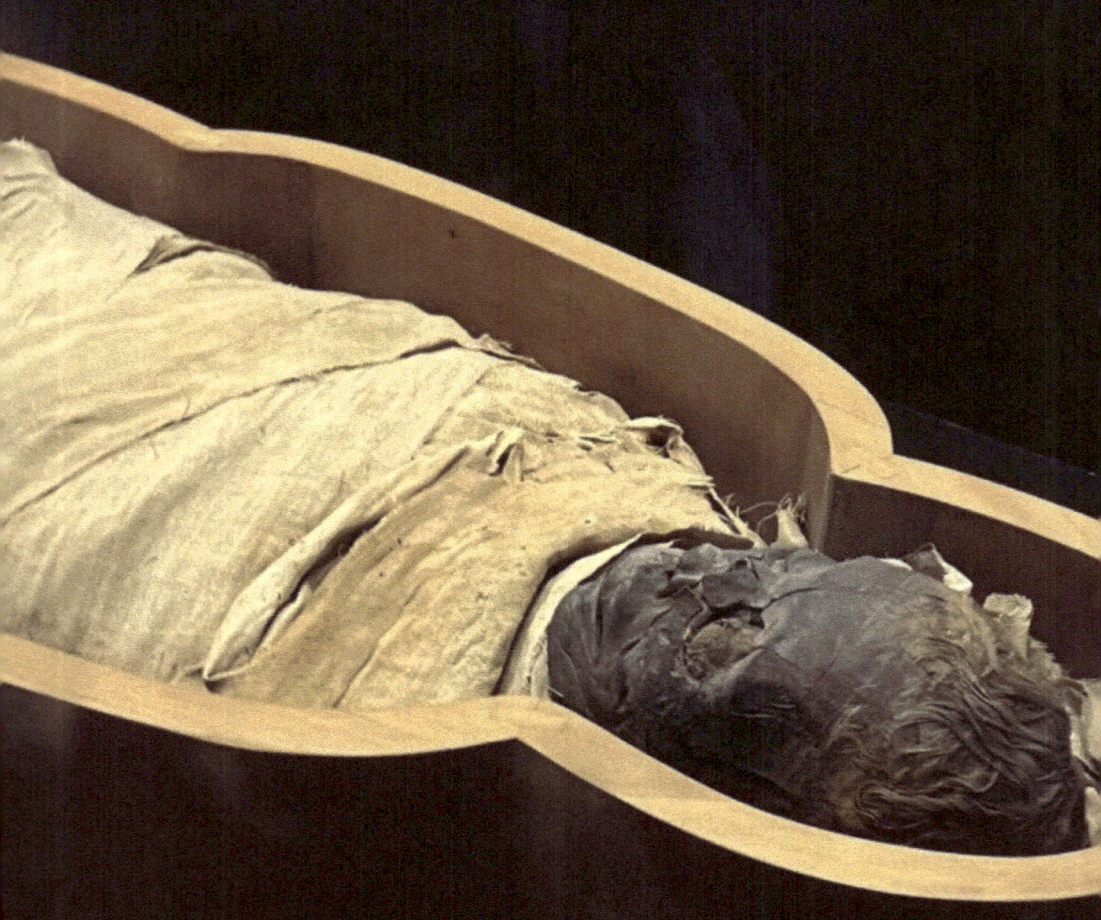

"*The practice of mummification in ancient Kemet, situated in the African Nile Valley, was a complex and significant ritual that evolved over thousands of years.*"

Queen Amenidis I at the Vatican Gregorian Museum, Photo by Daniel Laroche, MD

CHAPTER SEVEN

MUMMIFICATION

Mummification in the Ancient African Nile Valley

T he practice of mummification in Ancient Kemet, situated in the African Nile Valley, was a complex and significant ritual that evolved over thousands of years. This process was deeply rooted in the Ancient Nile Valley Africans' beliefs about death and the afterlife, reflecting their cultural and religious values.

Origins and Significance

Mummification began during Kemet's Old Kingdom period, around 2600 BCE, and continued for over 2,000 years into the Roman Period. The Ancient Nile Valley Africans believed that preserving the body was crucial for the deceased's journey into the afterlife. They viewed death not as an end, but as a transition to another realm where the soul would be judged by Ausar.

The Mummification Process

The mummification process was intricate and time-consuming, typically taking about 70 days to complete. The main steps included:

1. **Purification**: The body was washed with sacred Nile water, symbolizing both practical cleansing and spiritual purification.

2. **Organ Removal**: Internal organs, except the heart, were removed through an incision in the left side of the abdomen. The brain was extracted through the nasal cavity using a long hook. Thus, this process indicates they most likely had a profound knowledge of human anatomy.

3. **Desiccation**: The body was covered with natron, a naturally occurring salt, for approximately 40 days to remove all moisture.

4. **Organ Preservation**: The removed organs were dried, wrapped, and placed in canopic jars or returned to the body cavity.

5. **Body Stuffing**: The body cavities were filled with various materials such as linen, sawdust, and aromatic substances like myrrh, cinnamon, and cassia.

6. **Anointing and Wrapping**: The body was anointed with oils and resins, then meticulously wrapped in linen bandages.

7. **Funerary Rituals**: Priests performed the "Opening of the Mouth" ceremony to symbolically restore the deceased's senses for the afterlife.

Materials Used in Mummification

The embalmers used a variety of materials, each serving specific purposes:

- **Natron**: A naturally occurring salt mixture crucial for dehydrating the body.

- **Resins and Oils**: Handled for preservation and aromatic purposes, including coniferous resin, myrrh, and cedar oil.

- **Beeswax and Bitumen**: Used for sealing and preservation.

- **Linen**: Operated in the task of wrapping the deceased body for mummification.

Social and Economic Aspects

The quality of mummification varied depending on the deceased's social status and wealth. The most elaborate and expensive methods were reserved for pharaohs and the elite, while simpler techniques were used for the less affluent.

Legacy and Scientific Value

The mummification techniques of Ancient African Nile Valley were so effective that modern scientists can still study these preserved bodies, gaining insights into Ancient Kemetic life, health, and culture. Mummies from over 3,000 years ago still retain recognizable features, including skin, hair, and even tattoos.

Mummification in the Ancient African Nile Valley was more than a preservation technique, but a complex ritual that reflected the people of the African Nile Valley ' deep-seated beliefs about life, death, and the afterlife. This practice has left an indelible mark on our understanding of ancient African Nile Valley civilization and continues to fascinate researchers and the public alike.

Funerary Equipment

According to an ancient religious concept of Egyptians, faith was called a 'House of Eternity" as it represented the residue of the deceased in the afterlife.

The body was embalmed and preserved in a sarcophagus, around which numerous necessary objects were placed for life and sustenance in the beyond. Many of the objects were those which had been used during the deceased's earthly life, while others were made expressly for the afterlife.

The food offerings found in containers would have guaranteed the survival of the 'ba' (soul) of the deceased in eternity. Likewise, the toiletries, perfume vessels, ointment jars, jewels, clothes, footwear, furniture, and ornaments were to satisfy their every need and ensure a serene hereafter.

The 'ba', symbolized by two arms raised (Ka), was regarded as a person's spiritual double, embodying the Egyptian concept of duality. Because there is no other way to translate it, 'ba' is called the 'life force', spirit, or soul. Khnum, the ram-headed Neter (God), worked a potter's wheel to construct the 'ba' as the physical body was being made. This did not mean the 'ba' and body were inseparable. The phrase "going to one's 'ba' " generally referred to dying. The 'ba' left the body to join its celestial creator after death.

The 'ba' required food and drink throughout its life. The family of the deceased sent gifts to ensure the survival of the 'ba' after the body was buried. The 'ba' was believed to cross between the afterlife and human worlds through the false doors. It signified each family's ancestors, carried down from generation to generation. However, the ' 'ba' of Neters and kings meant individuality. A little figure with the 'ba' symbol and Heru name on its head represented the ruler. The king's 'ba' and the god's Heru name may have been related.

The so-called 'scenes from daily life' were often carved and painted on the walls of tombs. They depicted a wide range of human activities such as baking, brewing beer, weaving, fishing, navigating, and boatbuilding. In addition to these images, wooden or stone models representing similar tasks were commonly included among the funerary equipment. Their purpose was to ensure that the deceased would enjoy a happy and prosperous existence in the afterlife.

While these ritual elements aimed to secure eternal well-being, the physical treatment of the body was equally central to the preparation for the afterlife. An advanced scientific understanding of human biology and frequent references to complicated afterlife notions are crucial. Although mummification is mostly extinct, the scientific expertise of its practices fascinates us and has influenced today's embalming methods.

Mesu Heru

Photo by Daniel Laroche, MD

The burial practices of Ancient African Nile Valley reflect a profound connection between religion, cosmology, and the afterlife. Among these practices, the use of canopic jars to preserve the internal organs of the deceased stands out as a significant ritual. These jars were more than containers; they embodied the spiritual protection and divine guardianship provided by the four sons of Heru (Horus), known as Mesu Heru, and their associated female deities.

The Sons of Heru and Their Protective Role

The four sons of Heru—Imsety, Hapi, Duamutef, and Qebehsenuef—were integral to Ancient African Nile Valley funerary traditions. Each son was linked to a specific organ removed during mummification and placed in a canopic jar. These jars were designed with lids shaped like the heads of these deities, symbolizing their protective role over the organs essential for the deceased's journey to the afterlife.

1. **Hapi (Baboon-headed):** Hapi represented the North and was responsible for safeguarding the lungs. His jar was protected by Nbt-het (Nephthys), a goddess associated with mourning and protection.

2. **Duamutef (Jackal-headed):** Representing the East, Duamutef guarded the stomach. His jar was under the protection of Nit (Neith), a goddess symbolizing creation and war.

3. **Imsety (Human-headed):** Imsety symbolized the South and protected the liver. He was guarded by Aset (Isis), one of Egypt's most revered goddesses, embodying motherhood and magic.

4. **Qebehsenuef (Falcon-headed):**Associated with the West, Qebehsenuef protected the intestines. His jar was safeguarded by Serket, a goddess linked to healing and protection against venomous creatures.

Spiritual Significance of Canopic Jars

The canopic jars were more than practical tools in the mummification process but held deep spiritual significance. Ancient Africans of the Nile Valley believed that preserving these organs was vital for ensuring the deceased's completeness in the afterlife. The jars also symbolized harmony between physical preservation and divine intervention, as each organ was entrusted to a son of Heru and his corresponding Neteru (Goddess) for eternal protection.

The jars were often crafted from materials like limestone, pottery, or alabaster, reflecting their sacred purpose. Over time, their design evolved—from simple lids in earlier periods to elaborate representations of the sons of Heru during the New Kingdom. Even when embalming techniques advanced to preserve organs within the body, pseudo canopic jars continued to be included in tombs as symbolic artifacts.

Cosmic Connections

The sons of Heru were more than protectors but also cosmic entities attached to cardinal directions and celestial realms. Their association with stars and regions of Ancient African Nile Valley further emphasized their role in maintaining cosmic balance. This connection reinforced their importance in guiding the deceased through the challenges of the afterlife.

The burial practices involving canopic jars illustrate how Ancient Africans of the Nile Valley intertwined spirituality, traditions, and science in their quest for immortality. The four sons of Heru and their protective Neteru (Goddess) played pivotal roles in ensuring that both physical remains and spiritual essence were safeguarded for eternity. Through this ritualistic preservation, Ancient Africans of the Nile Valley expressed their belief in life after death—a cornerstone of their civilization's enduring legacy.

CHAPTER EIGHT
COFFINS, COFFIN TEXTS, AND USHABTI

The **Coffin Texts** are a collection of Ancient Nile Valley funerary spells that were written on coffins, beginning in the First Intermediate Period, dating back to 2100 BCE. They are partially derived from the earlier Pyramid Texts and reserved for royal use only but contained substantially new material related to everyday desires, which indicated a new target audience of common people. Ordinary Kemetians (ancient Egyptians) who could afford a coffin had access to the funerary spells, meaning the pharaoh no longer held exclusive rights to an afterlife.

The Outside of a Nile Valley Coffin of Queen Amenirdis I Photo by Daniel Laroche, MD

Ushabti figures—also spelled shabti or shawabty—are small statuettes made of wood or stone, often found in large numbers in Ancient Nile Valley tombs. The figures range in height from approximately 4 to 20 inches (10 to 50 cm) and often hold hoes in their arms.

They served as symbolic substitutes for the deceased, performing menial tasks in the afterlife at the command of the Neters (Gods). The word ushabti is usually translated as 'answerer'. In the New Kingdom (1539–1075 BCE), ushabti were fashioned to resemble the tomb owner, often in mummy form and inscribed with the owner's name.

Ushabti in Medu Neter

Figure 1: Ushabti, from the Tomb of Seti I,
son of Ramesses I, Photo by Daniel Laroche, MD

CHAPTER NINE

"BOOK OF COMING FORTH BY DAY"

Misnamed as Book of the Dead, Photo by Daniel Laroche, MD

The ***Book of the Dead*** is an Ancient Nile Valley funerary text, typically written on papyrus and used from the beginning of the New Kingdom (c. 1550 BCE to 50 BCE). Its original Nile Valley name translates as the Book of Coming Forth by Day or the Book of Emerging Forth into the Light. The term 'Book' best describes this loose collection of texts, intended to assist the deceased on their journey through the Duat (underworld) and into the afterlife. Many priests contributed to these texts over a span of nearly 1,000 years. Karl Richard Lepsius introduced the German name Todtenbuch (modern Totenbuch), which translates into English as Book of the Dead. Karl Richard Lepsius introduced the German name of the texts, *Todtenbuch,* (modern spelling *Totenbuch*), which translates to the *"Book of the Dead"* in English.

Boats in the Ancient African Nile Valley

The people of the Ancient Nile Valley traveled to distant lands in boats. Photo by Daniel Laroche, MD

Boats played a pivotal role in Ancient African Nile Valley, serving as essential tools for transportation, fishing, trade, and traditional practices. Evidence of their use dates back thousands of years, highlighting significant advancements in maritime technology.

Early Evidence of Nile Boats

The earliest known depiction of a Nile Valley boat appears on a granite pebble carving from the Khartoum Mesolithic layer (7050–6820 BCE). This artifact depicts a vessel more advanced than a simple canoe, incorporating features such as steering systems. These boats were likely used for fishing and transportation along the Nile.

Studies suggest these Mesolithic boats were designed for catching large species such as the Nile Perch, requiring vessels both sturdy and maneuverable.

Types of Boats

Papyrus Rafts:

Made from papyrus reeds, these rafts were ideal for navigating the calm waters of the Nile. They gained spiritual significance due to their association with the sun Neter (God) and were used for practical purposes such as hunting and fishing.

Wooden Boats:

Wooden vessels replaced papyrus rafts over time due to their durability and efficiency. They were used for transporting heavy materials like stones and obelisks for construction projects.

Papyriform Boats:

These wooden boats retained the shape of papyrus rafts to symbolize royalty and divinity. They were used for ceremonial purposes, including funerary rites and religious pilgrimages.

Technological Advancements

Early African Nile Valley boats demonstrated innovative designs, transcending simple reed rafts. The Khartoum Mesolithic pebble carving indicates refined architectural features that influenced Egyptian shipbuilding in later periods.

By the First Dynasty, around 3100 BCE, true planked hull construction emerged, marking a significant leap in nautical engineering.

1. Cultural and Economic Impact

Boats facilitated large-scale fishing, agriculture, and trade along the Nile. They enabled the movement of goods and people across vast distances, fostering economic growth and cultural exchange. Additionally, their symbolic association with Neteru (Deities) and royalty underscored their importance in traditional African Nile Valley ceremonies.

The Khufu ship is an intact, full-size solar barque from the Nile Valley. It was sealed in a pit alongside the Great Pyramid of Pharaoh Khufu around 2500 BC, during the Fourth Dynasty of the ancient Nile Valley Old Kingdom. Like other buried Ancient Nile Valley ships, it was part of the extensive grave goods intended for use in the afterlife.

The Khufu ship is one of the oldest, largest, and best-preserved vessels from antiquity. It is 43.4 meters (142 ft.) long and 5.9 meters (19 ft.) wide and is the world's oldest intact ship. It has been described as *"a masterpiece of woodcraft"* that could sail today, if put into a lake or a river. The ship was preserved in the Giza Solar Boat Museum but was moved to the Grand Egyptian Museum in August 2021.

Boats in the Ancient African Nile Valley were not only practical tools but also cultural artifacts that reflected technological ingenuity and societal values. From simple reed rafts to advanced wooden ships, they played a crucial role in shaping life along the Nile.

Uraeus

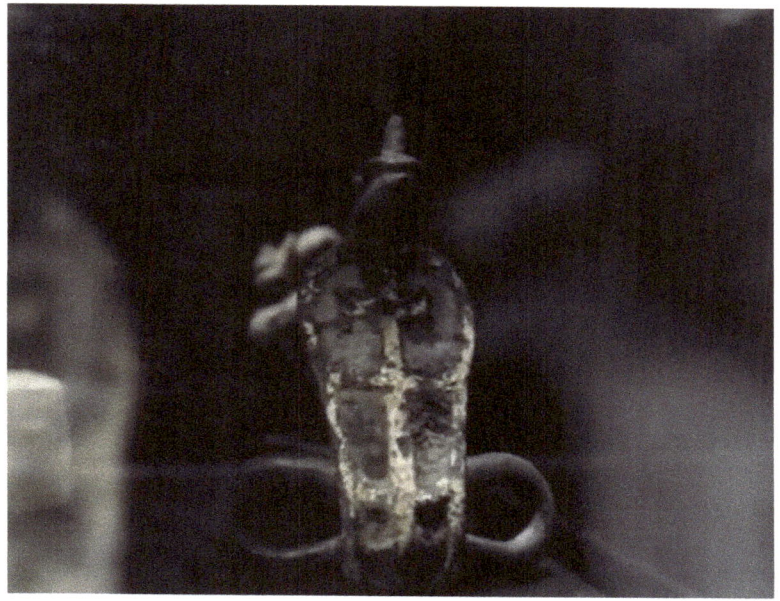

Uraeus Serpent, Photo by Daniel Laroche, MD

The Uraeus serpent was a central symbol in the Ancient African Nile Valley, where it represented divine authority, royal power, and protection. Its significance can be understood through its association with the cobra Neter Wadjet and its role in pharaonic regalia and religious iconography.

Symbolism and Religious Significance

- **Wadjet, the Cobra Neter:** The Uraeus symbolized Wadjet, one of Egypt's earliest deities and the protector of Lower Kemet. Depicted as a rearing cobra, Wadjet embodied both danger and protection, making her an ideal guardian for the pharaohs. Her fiery attributes, such as the ability to spit flames or venom, were mythologically linked to her role as a protector of the king and the kingdom.

- **Cosmic Order**: The Uraeus was associated with Ra, the sun Neter. It symbolized the "fiery eye" of Ra, linking the pharaoh to cosmic power and divine vision. This connection reinforced the pharaoh's role as an intermediary between Neters and humans, tasked with maintaining Ma'at (cosmic order).

Role in Royal Power

- **Pharaonic Regalia**: The Uraeus was prominently displayed on the crowns and headdresses of pharaohs. It served as a visual marker of sovereignty and divine legitimacy. The presence of the Uraeus on a pharaoh's crown indicated their divine protection by Wadjet and his authority over both Upper and Lower Kemet.

- **Symbol of Unification**: The Uraeus was often paired with the vulture Neter Nekhbet, representing Upper Kemet. Together, they symbolized the unification of Upper and Lower Kemet under a single ruler. This duality reinforced the idea of balanced governance over a unified kingdom.

Cultural Impact

- **Protection and Power**: Beyond its royal connotations, the Uraeus also symbolized protection for all of Kemet. Its menacing posture evoked fear in enemies while offering security to those under its care. This duality reflected broader Kemetic beliefs about serpents as both dangerous creatures and protective forces[1].

- **Artistic Depictions**: The Uraeus was a recurring motif in Ancient African Nile Valley art, appearing on crowns, amulets, and temple carvings. The enduring presence of Uraeus highlighted its importance as a cultural and religious emblem.

In summary, the Uraeus serpent encapsulated themes of divine authority, protection, unification, and cosmic order in Ancient Egyptian civilization. Its integration into royal iconography underscored its role as a potent symbol of pharaonic legitimacy and governance.

Figurine Depiction of a Serapium
Photo by Daniel Laroche, MD

Antinous as the Apis Bull,
Photo by Daniel Laroche, MD

CHAPTER TEN
SERAPEUM

The Serapeum was a religious institution dedicated to Serapis, a syncretic Greco-African deity established during the Ptolemaic period. Serapis combined elements of the African Neters, Osiris and Apis, with Greek influences such as Zeus or Hades, who symbolized healing, fertility, and the afterlife. The cult of Serapis was introduced to unify African and Greek beliefs under Ptolemaic rule.

Key Features of the Serapeum

- **Construction**: The most famous Serapeum was built in Alexandria by Ptolemy III Euergetes between 246–222 BCE. It stood on a rocky plateau, overlooking the sea, and serving as a cultural as well as religious center.

- **Functions**: These temples were pilgrimage sites for healing, fertility rites, and spiritual connection. They also housed large collections of books, making them centers of learning.

- **Architecture**: The Serapeum in Alexandria featured grand columns, subterranean galleries for mysteries, and bilingual inscriptions in Greek and hieroglyphs, emphasizing its cultural significance.

Roman Influence and Hadrian's Role

Under Roman rule, Egypt retained its importance as a province. Emperor Hadrian, with his lover Antinous, visited the Serapeum during his tour of the African Nile Valley in 130 CE with his lover Antinous. After Antinous drowned in the Nile, he was deified by local priests who associated him with Osiris and Serapis. Hadrian honored him by founding Antinoöpolis, integrating Greek and African cultures.

Decline and Destruction

The Serapeum faced destruction during the rise of Christianity. In 391 CE, Emperor Theodosius I issued an edict banning pagan worship. A Christian mob stormed the Serapeum of Alexandria, destroying its statues and artifacts. This marked a turning point in the decline of Ancient African spiritual practices.

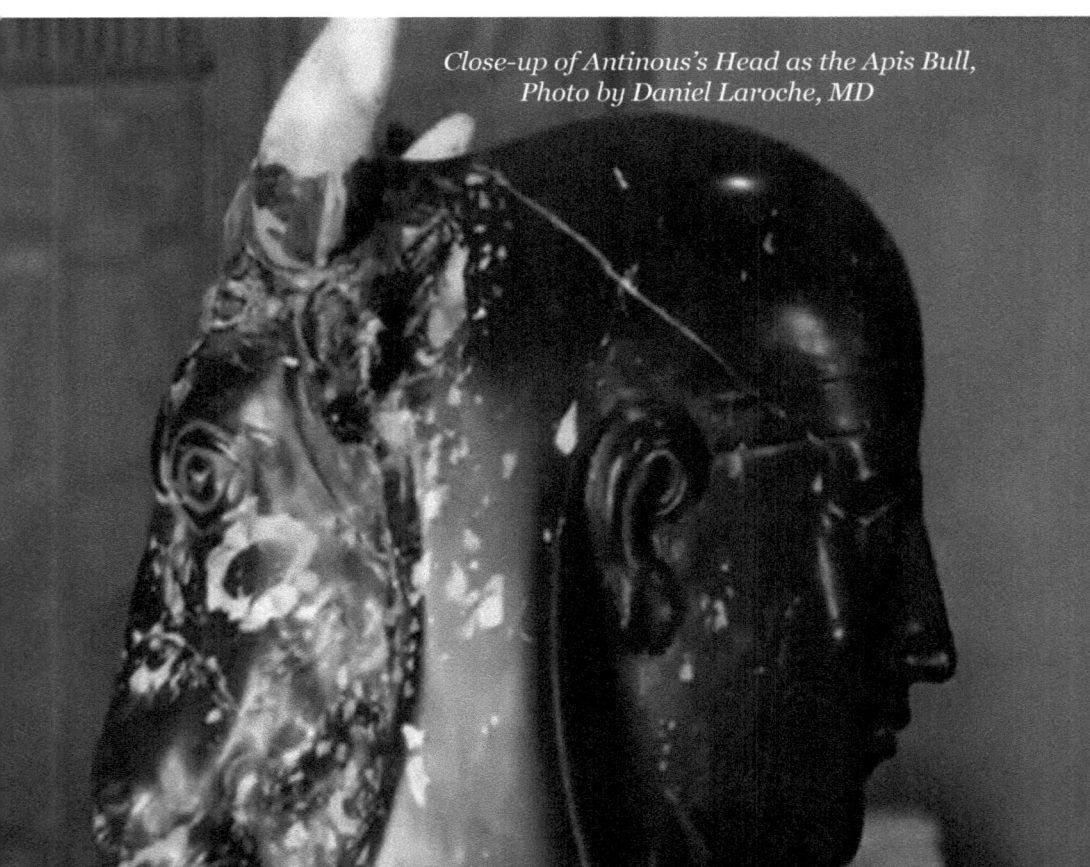

Close-up of Antinous's Head as the Apis Bull, Photo by Daniel Laroche, MD

Photo by
Daniel Laroche, MD

Antinous (110-130 CE) was a youth of Bithynia, who became the beloved of the Roman Emperor Hadrian (76-138 CE/117-138 CE) from around the age of 13, until his death around the age of 20.

All the ancient sources support that Antinous was nearly 20 when he drowned in the Nile River in October 130 CE, while accompanying Hadrian on a tour of the Nile Valley. After his death, Hadrian had him deified and in his admiration built on the Nile Valley shore, the city of Antipolis, also spelled 'Antinoöpolis'. A following soon developed and spread quickly. As a new god, Antinous became quite popular, and followers associated him with the Egyptian deity Ausar.

Antinous was almost instantly revered as a dying and reviving god, a deity who dies and returns to life for the good of humanity. Some sort of personal salvation was involved in the beliefs of the cult, which increased rapidly from Egypt throughout the provinces of the Roman Empire.

"All the ancient sources agree that Antinous was nearly twenty when he drowned in the Nile River in October 130 CE, while accompanying Hadrian on his tour of the Nile Valley."

Hapi European Depiction of Neter (God) of the Nile in Fountain Form Rome First Century AD, Photo by Daniel Laroche, MD

HAPI

The Neter Hapi: Fertility and Sustenance in the African Nile Valley

Hapi, the deity of the Nile's inundation, holds a central place in the mythology and culture of the Ancient African Nile Valley. Revered as a symbol of fertility and sustenance, Hapi was more than a Neter but a personification of the life-giving forces of the river that shaped one of the world's most enduring civilizations.

Role and Significance

Hapi was associated with the annual flooding of the Nile, an event that deposited fertile silt along its banks, enabling agriculture in an otherwise arid desert environment. This inundation, known as the "Arrival of Hapi," was vital for Egypt's agricultural prosperity and economic stability. The Ancient Nile Valley Africans believed Hapi controlled this essential phenomenon, making him a deity of profound importance. His titles, such as "Lord of the Fish and Birds of the Marshes" and "Lord of the River Bringing Vegetation," reflect his connection to the abundance provided by the Nile.

In addition to his role in agriculture, Hapi symbolized cosmic balance and harmony. He was considered a nurturing figure who maintained order in the universe, earning him recognition as "father of the gods." Despite his significance, Hapi was not worshipped as part of Egypt's formal theological systems but was widely celebrated through hymns, rituals, and offerings. His traditions centered on Elephantine Island near Aswan. The priests there used a nilometer to monitor water levels and predict floods throughout the Nile Valley.

Iconography

Hapi's depiction is unique among African Nile Valley deities. He is portrayed as an androgynous figure with pendulous breasts and a rounded belly, symbolizing fertility and nourishment. His blue or green skin represents water, while his adornments vary by region—papyrus plants for Lower Kemet and lotus flowers for Upper Kemet. These symbols emphasize his role in uniting Upper and Lower Kemet (Egypt). In some depictions, Hapi appears as twin figures tying together plants to symbolize this union.

Hapi's association with fertility extended beyond agriculture to broader spiritual concepts. He was linked to Nun, the primordial waters from which creation emerged, thereby connecting him to other cosmic forces like Ra, the sun god. This link reinforced his status as a divine provider and sustainer.

Cultural Impact

The Nile's centrality to ancient people of Kemet's life elevated Hapi's importance in both practical and spiritual realms. Ceremonies honoring Hapi were conducted to ensure successful floods and bountiful harvests. The river itself was seen as a divine gift, with its waters used in purification rituals and religious festivals. Hapi's influence persisted even during periods of religious reform. For instance, Akhenaten's attempts to promote Aten did not diminish Hapi's reverence among Africans of the Nile Valley.

Moreover, myths surrounding Hapi underscore his role in sustaining civilization. Alongside gods like Khnum, Satet, and Anuket—collectively known as the Elephantine Triad—Hapi was believed to reside near the Nile's source at Aswan, regulating its flow and ensuring its bounty.

Legacy

Hapi's legacy is inseparable from the Nile Valley civilization itself. As a symbol of fertility, sustenance, and unity, he embodied the essential forces that allowed Kemet to thrive for millennia. His image continues to remind us of humanity's deep connection with natural resources and their role in shaping cultural identities.

Through his portrayal as an intersex figure and his centrality in rituals tied to agriculture and cosmic balance, Hapi represents both physical sustenance and spiritual harmony—a testament to the profound respect Ancient Africans of the Nile Valley held for their environment.

A Roman Marble Statue of the Nile Valley Neter Anubis
Photo by Daniel Laroche, MD

The Roman adoption and transformation of the Ancient Kemetic (Egyptian) *Neters*—divine principles or deities—can be exemplified in the syncretism between Anubis and Mercury, particularly through the symbol of the caduceus. This process reflects how Romans integrated African spiritual and cultural elements into their own pantheon and iconography.

Mercury and Anubis

- Mercury, the Roman equivalent of Hermes, inherited many attributes from Greek mythology, including his role as a psychopomp (guide of souls to the underworld). This role closely parallels that of Anubis in Ancient African Nile Valley spiritual tradition. Anubis was responsible for guiding souls and overseeing mummification.

- The Romans identified Mercury with Anubis because of their shared affiliation with the afterlife. This integration demonstrates how Roman religion absorbed elements of the Ancient African Nile Valley, reinterpreting them within the structure of their religious thought.

The Caduceus

- The caduceus, a staff entwined with two serpents and often surmounted by wings, became a defining symbol of Mercury. Its origins trace back to Hermes in Greek mythology, where it symbolized peace, commerce, and negotiation. In one myth, Hermes used his staff to end a fight between two snakes, leading them to entwine peacefully around it.

- The caduceus may have deeper roots in Mesopotamian iconography, specifically the Sumerian god Ningishzida's staff with two intertwined serpents. This suggests that the symbol underwent transformations as it migrated through different cultures.

- In Roman iconography, Mercury is depicted holding the caduceus as a representation of his roles in communication, commerce, and guiding souls. The symbol also became associated with diplomacy and restoration.

Syncretism and Cultural Transformation

The Romans practiced *interpretatio romana*, a method of identifying foreign gods as manifestations of their own deities. This approach allowed them to incorporate diverse cultural elements into their religious system:

- Mercury's identification with Anubis reflects this syncretic process, blending Egyptian funerary traditions with Roman beliefs about boundaries and transitions between worlds.

- The transformation of symbols like the caduceus illustrates how ancient motifs were adapted to fit new cultural contexts, while retaining their core meanings of balance and regeneration.

Roman religion evolved through the adoption and reinterpretation of foreign deities and symbols, resulting in a rich tapestry of interconnected mythologies.

Ptolemy II

*Statue of King
Ptolemy II (285-264 BC)
Photo by Daniel
Laroche, MD*

Ptolemy II Philadelphus (309–246 BCE) was the second ruler of the Ptolemaic Dynasty in Egypt, reigning from 282 to 246 BCE. His rule marked a golden age for the kingdom, characterized by significant cultural achievements, economic prosperity, and strategic diplomacy. Born on the island of Kos to Ptolemy I Soter and Berenice I, Ptolemy II inherited a kingdom founded by his father, a former general of Alexander the Great. His reign consolidated these foundations and expanded Egypt's influence across the Mediterranean and beyond.

Ptolemy II embraced several African traditions, particularly those rooted in Ancient African Nile Valley culture and spirituality.

To strengthen his rule and integrate himself into the fabric of Kemetic society, Ptolemy II embraced:

- **Pharaonic Ideology and Religious Integration** Ptolemy II presented himself as a traditional Kemetic pharaoh, performing rituals and supporting the Kemetic priestly elite. He commemorated his activities in stelae, such as the Mendes stele, which recorded his worship of the ram god Banebdjedet, and the Pithom stele, which marked his inauguration at the temple of Pithom. He also emphasized traditional Pharaonic virtues, such as recovering spiritual statuary from foreign enemies.

- **Temple Construction and Restoration**: Ptolemy II financed large-scale temple projects across Kemet, including the construction of the core of the Temple of Isis at Philae and work on temples dedicated to Ancient African Nile Valley Neteru like Heru, Min, and Anhur-Shu. The contributions of Ptolemy II expose his patronage of Ancient African Nile Valley traditions and demonstrated his respect for them.

- **Fusion of Greek and African Nile Valley traditions:** He promoted syncretic religious practices, such as the establishment of the Serapis cult in Memphis. This cult blended Greek and African Nile Valley traditions, appealing to both communities.

These actions reflected Ptolemy II's strategic adoption of African traditions to legitimize his rule and foster unity within the diverse population of Ptolemaic Egypt.

Torso of the Neter Bull Apis, New Kingdom,
(1550-1070 BC), Photo by Daniel Laroche, MD

Photo by Daniel Laroche, MD

The Apis bull, one of the most revered sacred animals in Ancient African Nile Valley traditions, signified divine strength, fertility, and kingship. Celebrated primarily at Memphis, it was considered the living embodiment of the Neter Ptah and later associated with Ausa (Osiris) after death. Here is a more comprehensive look at its significance:

Role and Tradition

- The Apis bull was chosen based on specific physical markings, such as a white triangular mark on its forehead and other unique patterns. It was believed to be miraculously conceived by a divine ray or moonbeam.

- As a living deity, the bull resided in luxury at its temple near Ptah's sanctuary in Memphis. It was treated as an oracle, with its movements interpreted as divine messages. Its breath was thought to cure diseases, and its presence brought blessings.

- Public processions and festivals celebrated the bull, including a seven-day holiday for the bull's birth.

Connection to Ptah and Kingship

- Apis was initially associated with Ptah, the creator deity and divine architect. The bull symbolized qualities like strength and virility, aligning it with kingship.

- The bull's association with kingship is evident in titles like "Strong Bull of his Mother Hathor," linking it to both royal power and fertility.

After Death: Osiris-Apis (Serapis)

- Upon death, the Apis bull was embalmed and buried in grand ceremonies at the Serapeum in Saqqara. Its death marked a period of mourning followed by a search for its successor.

- During the Ptolemaic period, the Apis bull fused with Osiris to form Serapis (or Osorapis), a composite deity uniting African and Greek traditions. Serapis represented more than just fertility and kingship but also healing, the afterlife, and solar attributes.

Cultural Legacy

- The followers of Serapis became prominent under Ptolemy I Soter as a means of unifying Greek and African traditions. The deity gained popularity in Alexandria and even spread to Roman territories.

- Archaeological discoveries at Saqqara revealed over 60 mummified bulls, interred in massive granite sarcophagi, emphasizing the enduring importance of this cult over centuries.

The Apis bull exemplifies how Ancient African spirituality intertwined divine symbolism with political power, evolving through dynastic changes while maintaining its central role in African spirituality.

Serapis, a syncretic deity, was created during the reign of Ptolemy I Soter (305–282 BCE) in the Ptolemaic Kingdom of Egypt to unify Greek and African Nile Valley cultures. He is combined elements of Kemetic deities Ausar and Apis with Greek gods such as Zeus, Hades, and Dionysus. Serapis symbolized divine authority, fertility, healing, and the afterlife, serving as a cultural bridge during a time of convergence between Hellenistic and Ancient African Nile Valley traditions.

The followers of Serapis gained prominence with the construction of the Serapeum in Alexandria during the reign of Ptolemy III Euergetes (246–222 BCE). The temple became a prominent center of worship and culture, blending Greek and African traditions. The Serapeum was renowned for its healing powers, fertility

rites, and it housed a library said to rival the Great Library of Alexandria.

Serapis' popularity extended beyond Kemet into Greece and Rome. By the First Century CE, his worship had spread widely throughout the Roman Empire. However, this came to an end in 391 CE when Emperor Theodosius I ordered the destruction of pagan temples, including the Serapeum. A Christian mob desecrated and demolished the temple, marking a significant turning point in the decline of Ancient African spiritual traditions and the rise of Christianity.

Today, remnants of the Serapeum, such as Pompey's Pillar, stand as a testament to its former grandeur and its role in ancient cultural and religious history[8].

FOUNDATION OF ROME

The legend of Romulus and Remus is a foundational myth of Ancient Rome, blending themes of divine intervention, fraternal conflict, and political ambition.

Photo by Daniel Laroche, MD

Origins and Birth: Romulus and Remus were said to be the twin sons of Rhea Silvia, daughter of King Numitor of Alba Longa, and Mars, the god of war. Numitor had been dethroned by his brother Amulius, who forced Rhea to become a Vestal Virgin to prevent her from bearing heirs. Despite this, Rhea gave birth to the twins. Amulius ordered them to be drowned in the Tiber River, but they survived after their basket washed ashore near the Palatine Hill. A she-wolf (or *lupa*, which could also mean a prostitute) nurtured them until they were found by Faustulus, a shepherd, and his wife Acca Larentia.

Founding of Rome: As adults, Romulus and Remus restored Numitor to the throne by overthrowing Amulius. They then decided to establish a city at the site where they had been saved. Disagreement arose over its location—Romulus favored Palatine Hill while Remus preferred Aventine Hill. Augury was used to settle the dispute, but tension escalated when Remus mocked Romulus by jumping over the walls he was building. Enraged, Romulus killed his brother and named the city Rome after himself.

Historical Context: The myth originated in the Fourth Century CE and was codified by Roman scholars like Marcus Terentius Varro in the First Century CE. Archaeological evidence from the Eighth Century CE suggests parallels between history and legend, such as remnants of boundary walls near Palatine Hill.

Legacy: The story of Romulus and Remus symbolizes Rome's resilience. The image of the she-wolf suckling the twins became an enduring emblem of Roman identity. Romulus is credited with establishing key institutions that laid the foundation for Roman governance and military strength. He also expanded Rome's population through both alliances and controversial acts, most notably the abduction of the Sabine women. These myths highlight Rome's blend of strength, ambition, and adaptability in forging a civilization.

CHAPTER ELEVEN

POPE GREGORY XVI: SECRETLY CELEBRATING THE AFRICAN NETERU AT THE VATICAN

The Gregorian Egyptian Museum, established in 1839 by Pope Gregory XVI, is a fascinating part of the Vatican Museums that showcases a rich collection of ancient African Nile Valley artifacts. Its creation reflects the Pope's deep interest in antiquities and African Nile Valley traditions, which started in the 19th-century following the decoding of hieroglyphics (Medu Neter) by Jean-François Champollion. The museum was curated by Luigi Ungarelli, an Egyptologist, who played a pivotal role in organizing the collection and interpreting its artifacts.

Portrait of Louis Marie Ungarelli (1779-1845),
Reproduce with permission Bridgeman images

I didn't expect to see ancient Egyptian (Kemetian) relics at the Vatican. After all, Popes have long claimed that the Egyptians and other Africans were pagans who worshiped so-called devilish, animal-headed gods of Satan. Especially in the early stages of European expansion, Popes condoned and legitimized the system of enslaving God's African people. Yet, amazingly, the presence of the Neteru—Ancient African Nile Valley god-like beings—can be found hidden within the Vatican itself. In fact, the Popes perform rituals that draw upon the Ka—the spiritual essence of the Nile Valley tradition—along with Shu, Neter of the air, and MAAT, the Netert representing the concepts of truth, justice, balance, order, harmony, law, and morality. Through these rituals, the Popes create a spiritual mingling and evoke an atmosphere deeply rooted in these ancient forces and they create a link and associate the spirit evoking environment.

The museum is housed in the Belvedere Palace, utilizing spaces that were once part of Pope Pius IV's apartments. Pope

Gregory XVI personally financed the acquisition of many artifacts, sourcing them from Roman antique markets, private collections, and archaeological expeditions. The collection includes mummies, papyri (such as the Book of the Coming forth by Day, also known as the Book of the Dead also know has Pert em Heru meaning Utterances for coming into the light, or becoming enlightened), sarcophagi, statues, and other items that reflect ancient African Nile Valley traditions and daily life practices. Some pieces even originate from Hadrian's Villa in Tivoli, showcasing how ancient African Nile Valley culture influenced Roman art and architecture.

Luigi Ungarelli (1779–1845), the museum's first curator, was a Barnabite priest and one of Italy's earliest Egyptologists. He collaborated with prominent figures like Champollion to study hieroglyphics and contributed significantly to the understanding of ancient African Nile Valley artifacts in Rome. Ungarelli's expertise extended to interpreting inscriptions on Rome's obelisks and promoting Egyptology as a scientific discipline.

The presence of ancient African artifacts in the Vatican may seem surprising given Christianity's historical condemnation of "pagan" practices associated with ancient Egypt. However, these collections reveal a complex relationship where the Church simultaneously critiqued and absorbed elements of ancient African Nile Valley culture. For example, symbols like the ankh—a representation of life in ancient African Nile Valley—were reinterpreted within Christian iconography, influencing designs such as the cross. This interplay underscores how ancient African Nile Valley spirituality and symbolism subtly permeated Christian art and thought.

*Ceremonial Implement in the Shape of an Ankh, ca. 1400–
1390 B.C. Faience. The Metropolitan Museum of Art, New York.
Theodore M. Davis Collection, Bequest of Theodore M. Davis,
1915 (30.8.30) reproduced with permission*

Pope Gregory the XVI was the head of the catholic church between 1831 and 1846. The fact that he spent tens of thousands of dollars of his own money to support his interest in ancient African Kemetic (name of the land now known as Egypt) artifacts, shows he was more serious about this tradition than we are today. The Gregorian Egyptian Museum not only preserves invaluable African Nile Valley artifacts but also embodies the Vatican's role in advancing Egyptology as a field of study. Pope Gregory XVI's dedication to this endeavor demonstrated his broader intellectual curiosity and commitment to cultural preservation.

"Pope Gregory the XVI ...

spent tens of thousands of dollars of

his own money to support his interest

in ancient African Kemetic artifacts."

Pope Gregory XVI

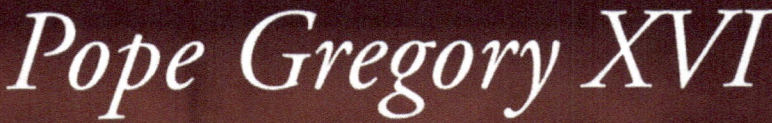

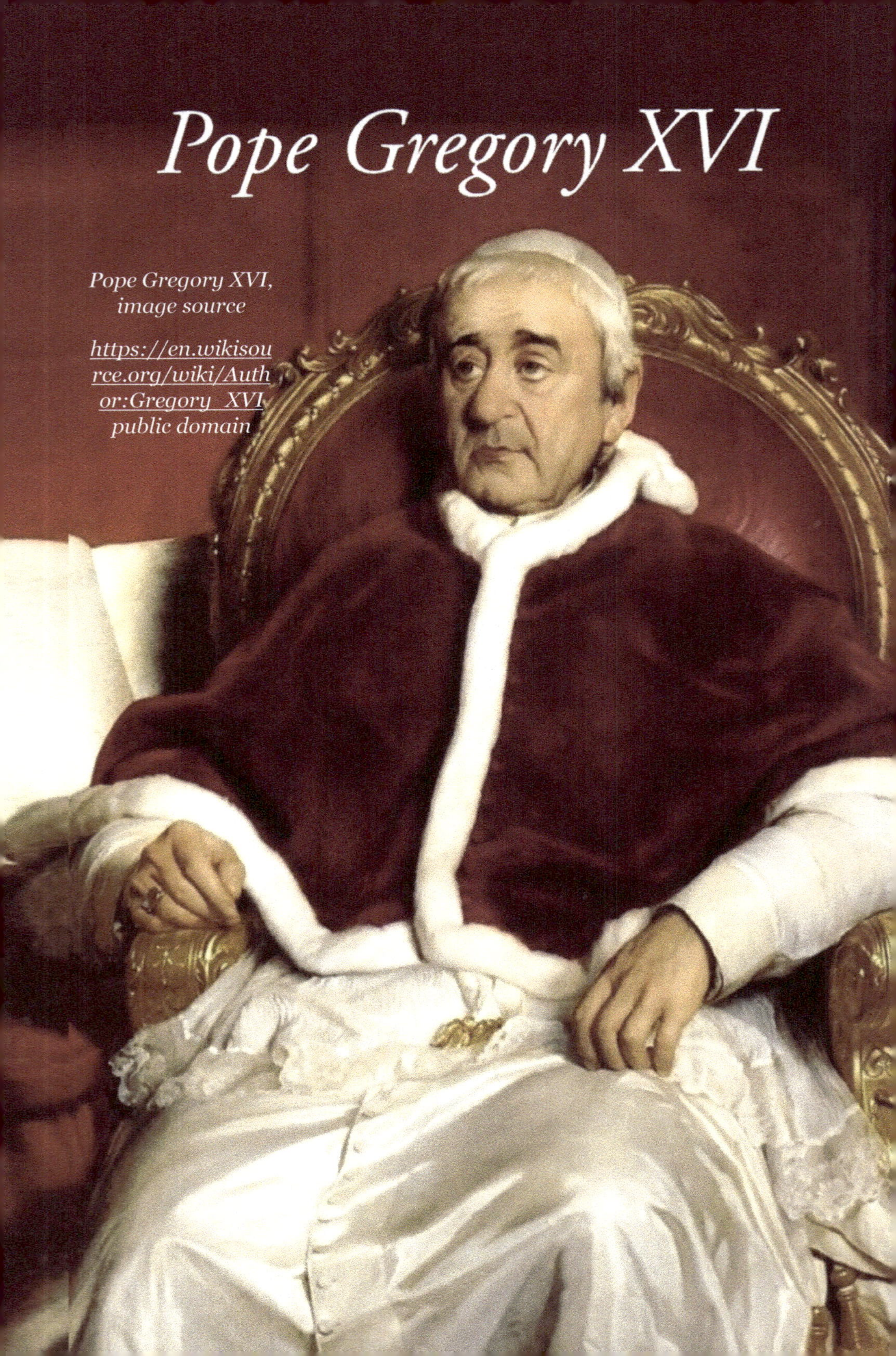

Pope Gregory XVI, image source

https://en.wikisource.org/wiki/Author:Gregory_XVI public domain

Pope Gregory the XVI funded 3 museums at the Vatican: 1) The Gregorian Etruscan Musuem in 1837, 2) The Gregorian Egyptian Museum in 1839 3) The Gregoriano Profano Museum in 1844. Pope Gregory the XVI even placed his name in a Shen (cartouche).

Image, Pope Gregory the XVI name in Medu Neter
at Gregorian Museum, image Daniel Laroche, MD.

The Pope wanted to immortalize his name like the Nsut Bity (pharaohs). The Pope had people that could read and write the African Nile Valley writings of the Medu Neter. The goal of the Popes, as leaders of the Catholic religion, was to live out and echo the imbued energy of the Neter by constructing a mirrored virtual reality—one in which they emulated the Neters and the Pharaohs through a worship that was both secret and openly expressed. Unfortunately, while doing so, they simultaneously broadcasted to their followers that the African Nile Valley traditions were pagan, heathen, and Ungodly.

Horemheb, 1374-1350 BC, is carried by soldiers on a carrying chair, behind and before them the Fan-bearer (Photo by: Bildagentur-online/Universal Images Group via Getty Images) reproduced with permission

The ostrich fan in ancient African Nile Valley, such as the one described in the Egyptian Museum (EA20767), holds significant cultural and symbolic value. It was not merely a practical object but also a representation of spiritual and social ideals.

The ostrich fan is associated with the concept of purification of the soul, aligning with Maat, the goddess of truth, balance, and cosmic order. Ostrich feathers symbolized purity and truth, as they were linked to Maat's feather used in the weighing of the heart ceremony in ancient African Nile Valley traditions.

The handle of this particular fan bears a carved depiction of Hathor's face with cow ears. Hathor was a goddess associated with love, music, and motherhood, further emphasizing the fan's sacred and ceremonial role.

Ostrich fan with Hathor with cows ears carved in ivory, British museum. EA20767, reproduced with permission.

Fans like these were included in tombs to provide comfort to the deceased and symbolically restore the "breath of life." They were also used to create shade, representing divine protection or presence.

Fan-bearers carried fans during royal processions and traditional ceremonies, underscoring their importance. The title "Wnmy n nsw" (Fan-bearer on the Right Side of the King) was an honorary position held by high-ranking officials. This role signified close proximity to the pharaoh, both physically and symbolically, as a trusted advisor or military leader.

The use of fans in ceremonial contexts extends beyond ancient African Nile Valley. In Vatican ceremonies, fan bearers (using flabella) accompany the Pope, evoking parallels with African Nile Valley pharaohs. This continuity highlights how symbols of authority and divinity have transcended cultures.

Pope with fan bearers, photo courtesy of
https://listverse.com/wp-content/uploads/2007/11/sedia.jpg

In summary, the ostrich fan served as a multifaceted symbol in ancient African Nile Valley—representing purification, divine protection, and elite status—while its ceremonial use resonates even in modern traditions like those of the Vatican.

Here is a picture of me in front of the Teken at the Vatican. Although there is a cross placed on the top, the foundation represents the Teken, symbolizing Ausar and concepts of resurrection, afterlife and mythology.

CHAPTER TWELVE

THE TEKEN AND THE ANKH

The Teken at the Vatican and the Meaning of the Ankh

The Tekhen, located in St. Peter's Square in Vatican City, is a remarkable artifact of African history. This towering monolith of red granite stands as a testament to human ingenuity, spiritual transformation, and historical continuity.

The obelisk, originally known in the Ancient African Nile Valley as "teken" or "tekhen" and now commonly called an obelisk," has deep spiritual and cultural significance, particularly in relation to the sun Neter Ra and the concept of divine kingship.

Origin of the Tekhen

Tekhens originated in Ancient Egypt around 2500 BC, with their prominence peaking during the New Kingdom period. These monumental structures were typically made from a single block of granite and featured a tapered design, culminating in a pyramidion at the top. The tekhen's shape symbolizes the sun's rays, representing a connection between the earth and the heavens. They were often placed at temple entrances to honor deities, particularly Ra, the sun Neter.

In Ancient African Nile Valley traditions, tekhens were seen as embodiments of light and were associated with creation myths. They were believed to be petrified rays of the sun, linking them to the divine. The construction of tekhen was often commissioned by pharaohs to commemorate their reigns and achievements, reinforcing their status as intermediaries between gods and humans.

Ausar, known as Osiris in Greek, was a key figure in Ancient African Nile Valley traditions, representing resurrection and the afterlife. While obelisks were primarily linked to Ra, they also connected the broader pantheon of Ancient African Nile Valley Neteru, including Ausar. The construction of the Tekhen often served dual purposes: honoring Neteru like Ra while simultaneously reinforcing the divine right of pharaohs who claimed descent from Ausar.

Tekhen were integral to various spiritual practices, symbolizing more than just political power but also spiritual beliefs. They were often inscribed with Medu Neter (hieroglyphs) that detailed the pharaoh's accomplishments and his relationship with the gods, including Ausar. This duality illustrates how tekhens functioned within both political and religious frameworks in Ancient African Nile Valley.

In summary, obelisks are monumental icons originating in Ancient Kemet (Egypt). They personify religious significance tied to solar traditions. They also assert the divine authority of rulers like Ausar through their inscriptions and placements in sacred spaces.

The Ankh: The Key of Life

The ankh, one of Ancient Africa's most iconic symbols, represents "life" or "breath of life." Its design—a looped cross—symbolizes both mortal existence and eternal life. The ankh was widely used in African art, frequently seen in the hands of Neteru, who presented it to pharaohs as a gesture of granting life or immortality. It also symbolized vital elements like air, water, and the sun.

In addition to its spiritual significance in Ancient Africa, the ankh was later adopted by Coptic Christians as a symbol of resurrection and eternal life. Known as the *crux ansata* (handled cross), it became a Christian emblem while retaining its original connotations of life and immortality. This adaptation highlights how symbols can transcend their original cultural contexts to acquire new meanings.

Symbolism and Legacy

Both the Tekhen and the ankh reflect profound aspects of Ancient African spirituality.

These symbols continue to captivate modern audiences, offering insights into humanity's enduring quest to understand life, death, and what lies beyond.

The **ankh**, often referred to as the "key of life," is a powerful and lasting symbol from Ancient Egypt. It represents life, immortality, and the union of opposites such as male and female or heaven and earth. It dates back to the Early Dynastic Period (c. 3150–2613 BCE) and was prominently featured in Ancient African Nile Valley art, religion, and funerary practices. The ankh was frequently depicted in the hands of deities like Ausar, Auset, and Ra, symbolizing their power to sustain life and grant eternal existence. It also appeared in burial chambers to ensure life after death.

The **Nile Valley civilization** was one of the earliest and most advanced societies in human history. Flourishing in the rich, fertile land bordering the Nile River, the Ancient Kemetians (Egyptians) achieved remarkable advancements in writing (Medu Neter), mathematics, medicine, engineering, astronomy, and architecture. They constructed monumental structures like pyramids and temples. They developed a 365-day calendar based on astronomical observations. Their greatness was also evident in a complex social hierarchy led by pharaohs regarded as divine.

The concept of **MAAT**, central to Ancient African Nile Valley philosophy, emphasized truth, balance, justice, and order. This moral framework guided their governance and societal norms. The tangible legacy of Nile Valley leaders is preserved through extensive archaeological evidence—artifacts, writings, monuments—unlike many biblical figures whose existence lacks physical evidence.

The **cultural influence** of Ancient African Nile Valley extended far beyond its borders. The ankh itself was later adapted by Coptic Christians into the *crux ansata* as a variant of the Christian cross. Many aspects of Egyptian civilization inspired subsequent cultures and religions.

The Gregorian Museum's highlights on Ancient African Nile Valley traditions serve as a reminder of this extraordinary legacy. It encourages continued exploration of the contributions made by African leaders in the Nile Valley civilization.

Additional References, Citations, and Readings

Chapter 2

[1]https://www.thearchaeologist.org/blog/the-false-doors-of-the-egyptian-tombs-a-threshold-between-the-worlds-of-the-living-and-the-dead

[2]https://www.tripsinegypt.com/blog/ancient-egyptian-civilization/false-doors-in-ancient-egypt/

[3]https://egyptatours.com/discover-the-false-doors-in-ancient-egypt/

[4] https://en.wikipedia.org/wiki/Mastaba

[5]   https://news.artnet.com/art-world/tomb-mastaba-egypt-2459275

[6]https://www.gbnews.com/science/archaeology-breakthrough-ancient-egypt-tomb-pharaoh-mystery

[7]https://africame.factsanddetails.com/article/entry-1099.html

[8] https://ancient-egypt-online.com/mastaba.html

[9] https://www.britannica.com/art/Egyptian-architecture

[10] https://en.wikipedia.org/wiki/Valley_of_the_Kings

[11]https://collections.mfa.org/objects/146374/false-door-stele-of-senwehem?ctx=a6cf618c-e7f1-45ee-9f7c-9f0701d49962&idx=411

[13]https://images.metmuseum.org/CRDImages/eg/original/DP351531.jpg?sa=X&ved=2ahUKEwjO69WNobqMAxUJl-4BHY3EIpUQ_B16BAgBEAI

[14]https://www.sidestone.com/books/the-architecture-of-mastaba-tombs-in-the-unas-cemetery

[15]https://www.iiad.edu.in/the-circle/history-of-egyptian-architecture/

[16] https://www.britannica.com/technology/mastaba

[17]https://www.artslookup.com/ancient/egyptian-architecture.html

[19]https://thebanmappingproject.com/articles/anatomy-tomb-ancient-and-modern-designations-chambers-and-features

[20] https://friesian.com/tombs.htm

[21]https://australian.museum/learn/cultures/international-collection/ancient-egyptian/tombs-in-ancient-egypt/

[22] https://www.metmuseum.org/met-publications/middle-kingdom-tomb-architecture-at-lisht-the-metropolitan-museum-of-art-egyptian-expedition

[23] https://en.wikipedia.org/wiki/False_door

[24]https://www.egypttoursportal.com/blog/egyptian-civilization/false-doors-in-ancient-egypt/

[25] https://ancientegyptonline.co.uk/falsedoor/

[26]https://www.egypttoursportal.com/en-us/blog/egyptian-civilization/false-doors-in-ancient-egypt/

[27] https://www.youtube.com/watch?v=9eSWuUGfIbk

[28]https://www.metmuseum.org/art/collection/search/543937

[29]https://africame.factsanddetails.com/article/entry-1060.html

[30]https://en.wikipedia.org/wiki/Ancient_Egyptian_architecture

[31]https://www.britannica.com/art/Egyptian-art/Architecture

Chapter 3

[1] https://historycooperative.org/ptah/

[3]https://www.penn.museum/collections/object/503391

[4]https://www.britishmuseum.org/collection/object/Y_EA37 899

[5] https://en.wikipedia.org/wiki/Khonsu

[6] https://www.ask-aladdin.com/all-destinations/egypt/category/ancient-egyptian-gods/page/khonsu-egyptian-moon-god

[7] https://en.wikipedia.org/wiki/Ptah

[8]https://www.metmuseum.org/art/collection/search/549247

[9] https://egypt-museum.com/stele-of-nakhtimen/

[10]https://www.albumonline.com/detail/en/MDY4ODUzMA/stela-dedicated-god-ptah-by-nakhtemmut-limestone-deir-medina-dynasty-alb11627394

[11] https://konouzeg.com/blog/post/the-whispering-god-how-ptah-spoke-the-universe-into-existence

[12] https://drvictorbodo.com/2024/08/10/the-magical-power-of-the-words-and-god-ptah/

[13]https://study.com/cimages/multimages/16/tri.jpg?sa=X&ved=2ahUKEwjaxMbD1bqMAxXzVPEDHa9_OgsQ_B16BAgJEAI

[14] https://www.thecollector.com/egyptian-god-ptah/

[15] https://www.artic.edu/artworks/12985/fragment-of-a-stela-of-neferhotep

[16] https://www.artic.edu/artworks/127859/stela-of-amenemhat-and-hemet

[17]https://www.worldhistory.org/image/4693/egyptian-stela-of-neferhotep/

[18]https://www.jstor.org/stable/community.27439208

[20] https://www.ingeniahistory.com/post/stelae-the-multifunctional-ancient-egyptian-markers

[21] https://oldworldgods.com/egyptians/khonsu-god-of-the-moon/

[24] https://www.britannica.com/topic/Khonsu

[25] https://study.com/learn/lesson/ptah-symbols-temples-role-in-egypt.html

[26] https://www.britannica.com/topic/Ptah

[27] https://ancientegyptonline.co.uk/ptah/

[28] https://egyptianmuseum.org/deities-ptah

[29]https://www.touregypt.net/featurestories/neferrenpet.htm

[30] https://egypt-museum.com/stela-of-neferhotep/

[31] https://www.wonderfulthingsart.com/post/offering-stela-of-neskhons

[32] https://journals.openedition.org/bifao/500

[33] https://www.wonderfulthingsart.com/post/iah-thoth-receiving-the-wadjet

[34]https://www.touregypt.net/featurestories/nakht.htm

[35]https://www.academia.edu/32571530/The_Stela_of_Nakht_Son_of_Nemty_Contextualizing_Object_and_Individual_in_the_Funerary_Landscape_at_Abydos

[36]https://egyptmuseum.egyptmuseum.com/post/774869097302441984/stele-of-nakhtimen

[37] http://egyptgrammar.rutgers.edu/Miscellany/min-nakht_zagreb.pdf

[38]https://www.ipernity.com/doc/laurieannie/24233359

[39] https://timelessmyths.com/gods/egyptian/khonsu

[40] https://ancientegyptonline.co.uk/khonsu/

[41] https://study.com/learn/lesson/khonsu-facts-symbols.html

[42] https://anthropologyreview.org/history/ancient-egypt/egyptian-god-of-the-moon/

[1] https://picryl.com/media/funerary-stele-of-nebsu-overseer-of-the-kings-aviaries-thebes-middle-kingdom-0d113d

[2]https://commons.wikimedia.org/wiki/File:Funerary_stele_of_Nebsu,_overseer_of_the_king's_aviaries,_Thebes,_Middle_Kingdom,_2040-1640_BC,_limestone_-_Museo_Gregoriano_Egizio_-_Vatican_Museums_-_DSC00783.jpg

[3]https://www.metmuseum.org/art/collection/search/544345

[4] https://www.jstor.org/stable/3854485

[5] https://artgallery.yale.edu/collections/objects/6941

[7]https://www.britishmuseum.org/collection/object/Y_EA1184

[8]https://commons.wikimedia.org/wiki/Category:Steles_of_the_Egyptian_12th_dynasty

Chapter 4

[1]https://utahutes.com/sports/mens-basketball/roster/ezra-ausar/15509

[2] https://en.wikipedia.org/wiki/Ausar

[3] https://en.wikipedia.org/wiki/Ausar_Thompson

[4] https://www.ausarmusic.com

Chapter 5

[1]   https://egymonuments.gov.eg/collections/offering-table-of-thutmose-iii/

[2]https://historicaleve.com/offering-tables-in-ancient-egypt/

[4]https://www.memphis.edu/egypt/events/images/offeringtable.pdf

[5]https://www.metmuseum.org/art/collection/search/569118

[6]https://antiquities.bibalex.org/Collection/Detail.aspx?collection=39&a=612&lang=en

[7] https://www.brooklynmuseum.org/objects/3954

[8] https://ancientegyptonline.co.uk/offeringformula/

Chapter 6

[1] https://en.wikipedia.org/wiki/Tuya_(queen)

[2] https://id.wikipedia.org/wiki/Ratu_Tuya

[3]https://www.museivaticani.va/content/museivaticani/en/collezioni/musei/museo-gregoriano-egizio/sala-v--statuario/statua-della-regina-tuia.html

[4] https://www.alamy.com/stock-photo/queen-tuya.html

[5]https://www.egypttoday.com/Article/4/41789/Queen-Tuya-wife-of-King-Seti-I-mother-of-King

[6]https://www.pinterest.com/pin/queen-tuya-and-princess-tia-by-bhansith-on-deviantart--503981014561722376/

[7]https://www.pinterest.com/pin/queen-tuya-queen-tuya-was-the-wife-of-pharaoh-seti-i-of-kemet-and-mother-of-princess-tia-ramesses-ii-and-henutmire-she--27443878972276826/

 [1]https://thesevenworlds.wordpress.com/2013/03/21/a-story-of-ausar-and-auset/

[2]https://open.spotify.com/intlid/track/1k5fcxZNZDRXvkc6hhWuVu

[3] https://www.youtube.com/watch?v=Y-Wiq4YgFPo

[4]   https://tunebat.com/Info/Auset-and-Nebhet-Labtekwon-Megan-Livingston-Wayna/1k5fcxZNZDRXvkc6hhWuVu

[5] https://www.instagram.com/artistmetu/p/CjJ2AO-jdon/

[6]https://fineartamerica.com/featured/nebthet-ausar-auset-artist-metu.html

[7]https://www.tiktok.com/@ubuntu.botho.spac/video/74496
53457335930118

[1] https://en.wikipedia.org/wiki/Anubis

[2]https://nationalgeographic.grid.id/read/134025282/anubis-
dewa-mitologi-mesir-kuno-penjaga-makam-firaun-
tutankhamun?page=all

[3] https://p2k.stekom.ac.id/ensiklopedia/Anubis

[4] https://id.wikibooks.org/wiki/Mesir_Kuno/Agama/Anubis

[5] https://id.wikipedia.org/wiki/Anubis

[6]https://www.instagram.com/komunitas_salihara/p/C-
pdKqfhv31/

[7] https://pixabay.com/id/images/search/anubis/

[8]https://www.youtube.com/watch?v=wi8-mHgbTfs

[1] https://ancientegyptonline.co.uk/serqet/

[2] https://en.wikipedia.org/wiki/Maahes

[3] https://en.wikipedia.org/wiki/Sekhmet

[4]https://www.worldhistory.org/article/885/egyptian-gods---
the-complete-list/

[5]   https://www.etsy.com/hk-en/listing/987223672/vintage-
maahes-statue-ancient-egyptian

[6]https://www.pinterest.com/pin/milky-rozen-on   instagram-
serket-goddess-of-medicine-and-poison-is-a-very-mysterious-
and-quiet-goddess-whose-presence-is-both-frightening-and-
reassuring-at-t-in-2024--1144547692796510772/

[7]   https://forum.infinitymu.net/threads/vd-uber-serket-set-
feb-22.137176/

[8] https://www.steamcardexchange.net/index.php

[1] https://veilofaset.com/wisdom/the-creation-of-bes/

[2] https://id.wikipedia.org/wiki/Amun

[3]https://www.human-earth.net/2017/04/magic egypt_18.html

[4] https://seshkemet.weebly.com/djehuty-thoth.html

[5] https://egyptianmuseum.org/deities-thoth

[6] https://books.google.ne/books?id=QPQxDwAAQBAJ

[7]https://www.threads.net/@temple_afrika/post/DBkOZXtS6 H8

1. https://papersowl.com/examples/sekhmets-statue-a-glimpse-into-ancient-egypts-heart/

2. https://en.wikipedia.org/wiki/Sekhmet

3. https://www.ipl.org/essay/Sekhmet-The-Egyptian-Goddess-Of-Healing-PKX3Q8QMUXPV

4. https://arce.org/resource/statues-sekhmet-mistress-dread/

5. https://orderwhitemoon.org/goddess/sekhmet-flames/Sekhmet.html
6. https://www.123helpme.com/essay/Sekhmet-Mythology-Essay-656122
7. http://www.gifteconomy.com/articlesAndEssays/journeyW ithSekhmet.html
https://www.thegoddessinside.com/goddess-diaries-blog/2016/9/21/the-power-of-sekhmet?format=amp

[1] https://en.wikipedia.org/wiki/Amenirdis_I

[2]https://laciviltaegizia.org/2023/01/19/alabaster-statue-of-amenirdis-i/

[3] https://id.wikipedia.org/wiki/Amenirdis_I

[4] https://pantheon.world/profile/person/Amenirdis_I

[5]https://isac.uchicago.edu/museum-exhibits/nubia/god%E2%80%99s-wives-amun

[6] https://artsandculture.google.com/entity/m06kfzj

[7] https://p2k.stekom.ac.id/ensiklopedia/Amenirdis_I

[8]https://artsandculture.google.com/entity/amenirdis-i/m06kfzj

Chapter 7

1. https://en.wikipedia.org/wiki/Canopic_jar
2. https://www.respectegypttours.com/blog/what-four-gods-were-associated-with-the-canopic-jars
3. https://www.metmuseum.org/art/collection/search/559935
4. https://en.wikipedia.org/wiki/Four_sons_of_Horus
5. https://www.spurlock.illinois.edu/exhibits/online/mummification/artifacts4
6. https://www.brooklynmuseum.org/objects/3562
7. https://www.historyforkids.net/canopic-jars.html
8. https://exhibitions.kelsey.lsa.umich.edu/jackal-gods-ancient-egypt/duamutef.php
9. https://ijahss.net/assets/files/1660760799.pdf
10. https://www.historyskills.com/classroom/year-7/mummification/
11. https://www.si.edu/spotlight/ancient-egypt/mummies
12. https://www.tripsinegypt.com/blog/ancient-egyptian-civilization/ancient-egyptian-mummification/
13. https://egittolizzando.altervista.org/wp-content/uploads/2020/08/A-Review-on-the-materials-used-During-mammification-process.pdf
14. https://discoveringegypt.com/egyptian-mummification/

15. https://en.wikipedia.org/wiki/Ancient_Egyptian_funerary_practices

16. https://english.elpais.com/culture/2023-02-02/new-research-reveals-rare-ingredients-that-ancient-egyptians-used-to-preserve-mummies.html

17. https://www.britannica.com/story/thats-a-wrap-methods-of-mummification

18. https://www.worldhistory.org/article/44/mummification-in-ancient-egypt/

19. https://www.nationalgeographic.com/premium/graphics/egypt-mummy-saqqara-excavation-golden-age-feature

20. https://www.readingmuseum.org.uk/blog/journey-afterlife-mummification-ancient-egypt

21. https://www.britishmuseum.org/collection/galleries/egyptian-death-and-afterlife-mummies

22. https://www.mpm.edu/sites/default/files/images/content/education/programs/curiosity/may/Mummification_Explained_v2.pdf

23. https://www.mylearning.org/stories/a-step-by-step-guide-to-egyptian-mummification
24. https://www.sciencedaily.com/releases/2020/12/201216134517.htm

25. https://www.spurlock.illinois.edu/exhibits/online/mummification/materials.html

26. https://www.pbs.org/wgbh/nova/peru/mummies/

27. https://science.howstuffworks.com/mummy1.htm

28. https://www.egypttoursportal.com/en-us/the-secret-of-egyptian-mummification/

29. https://www.ebsco.com/research-starters/religion-and-philosophy/ancient-egyptian-afterlife-beliefs

30. https://www.worldhistory.org/article/914/cultural--theological-background-of-mummification/

31. https://library.fiveable.me/gods-graves-and-pyramids-ancient-egyptian-religion-and-ritual/unit-9

32. https://africame.factsanddetails.com/article/entry-1102.html

33. https://bartonfuneral.com/funeral-basics/history-of-embalming/

Chapter 8

[1] https://en.wikipedia.org/wiki/Ushabti

[2]https://smarthistory.org/ushabti-ancient-egyptian-afterlife/

[3] https://www.shabtis.com/ss.php

[4] https://www.ancientegyptblog.com/?p=1922

[5]https://www.ucl.ac.uk/museumsstatic/digitalegypt/burialcustoms/shabtispell.html

[6] https://ancientegyptonline.co.uk/shabti/

[7]https://www.ucl.ac.uk/museumsstatic/digitalegypt/literature/religious/bd6.html

[8] https://mollybrown.org/ushabti/

Chapter 9

1. https://www.respectegypttours.com/blog/nile-cobra-in-egyptian-tales

2. https://worldhistoryedu.com/uraeus-in-ancient-egypt/

3. https://en.wikipedia.org/wiki/Uraeus

4. https://study.com/academy/lesson/egyptian-uraeus-definition-symbol-meaning.html

5. https://egyptianimports.com/blogs/news/cobras-in-ancient-egypt-symbols-of-power-and-protection

6. https://scholarworks.uvm.edu/context/hcoltheses/article/1278/viewcontent/Argyros_Thesis.pdf

[1] https://en.wikipedia.org/wiki/Nile_boat

[2] https://www.wikiwand.com/en/articles/Nile_boat

[3] http://www.taneter.org/nile.maritime.html

[4] https://www.touregypt.net/featurestories/aboat.htm

[5]https://thetidesofhistory.com/2019/06/16/ships-of-history-early-boats-egypt-the-nile/

Chapter 10

1. https://www.worldhistory.org/Serapis/

2. https://www.encounterstravel.com/blog/serapeum-of-alexandria

3. https://archiv.ub.uni-heidelberg.de/propylaeumdok/3691/1/Pfeiffer_The_god_Serapis_2008.pdf

4. https://en.wikipedia.org/wiki/Serapis

5. https://www.egypt-uncovered.com/blog/the-serapeum-of-alexandria

6. https://www.worldhistory.org/Ptolemaic_Egypt/

7. https://www.historyskills.com/classroom/ancient-history/serapis/

1. https://www.encounterstravel.com/blog/serapeum-of-alexandria

2. https://www.egypt-uncovered.com/blog/the-serapeum-of-alexandria

3. https://madainproject.com/serapeum

4. https://worldqueerstory.wordpress.com/2020/11/08/hadrian-and-antinous/

5. https://traveltoeat.com/pompeys-pillar-and-the-serapeum-alexandria-egypt/

6. https://en.wikipedia.org/wiki/Serapeum_of_Alexandria

7. https://www.metmuseum.org/essays/roman-egypt

8. https://en.wikipedia.org/wiki/Antinous

9. https://www.academuseducation.co.uk/post/hadrian-and-antinous

10. https://www.britannica.com/topic/Serapis

11. https://the-past.com/feature/antinoopolis-why-did-emperor-hadrian-build-a-city-in-egypt/

12. https://www.britannica.com/place/ancient-Egypt/Roman-and-Byzantine-Egypt-30-bce-642-ce

13. https://en.wikipedia.org/wiki/Antino%C3%B6polis

14. https://ancient-egypt-online.com/romans.html

15. https://www.antinopolis.org/antinoopolis.html

16. https://serapeaegypt.commons.gc.cuny.edu/a-brief-history/worship/

17. https://www.britannica.com/topic/Serapeum

18. https://www.ostia-antica.org/regio3/17/17-4.htm

19. https://etc.worldhistory.org/travel/the-obelisk-of-antinous-2/

20. https://en.wikipedia.org/wiki/Hadrian

21. https://antigonejournal.com/2022/02/looking-for-antinous/

22. https://antigonejournal.com/2024/06/hadrians-villa-and-its-treasures/

23. https://www.reddit.com/r/lgbthistory/comments/waxkhv/antinous_lover_of_the_roman_emperor_hadrian/

24. https://www.worldhistory.org/Roman_Egypt/

25. https://en.wikipedia.org/wiki/Temple_of_Isis_and_Serapis

26. http://www.sacred-destinations.com/egypt/alexandria-serapeum

27. https://www.historyskills.com/classroom/ancient-history/serapis/

28. https://ncse.ngo/temple-serapis

29. https://erevistas.uc3m.es/index.php/ARYS/article/download/4504/3360/

30. https://en.wikipedia.org/wiki/Hapi_(Nile_god)

31. https://kids.britannica.com/students/article/Hapi/311035

32. https://www.landofpyramids.org/hapi.htm

33. https://malaikamutere.com/2019/02/23/hapis-shero-journey/

34. https://papersowl.com/examples/the-ancient-egyptian-civilization/

35. https://www.123helpme.com/essay/Role-Of-Hapi-In-Ancient-Egypt-PJAUYMHPUV

36. https://www.britannica.com/topic/Hapi

37. https://study.com/academy/lesson/hapi-origin-mythology-egyptian-god-nile.html

38. https://en.wikipedia.org/wiki/Romulus_and_Remus

39. https://www.reddit.com/r/AskHistorians/comments/48jvlp/is_there_any_veracity_to_the_romulus_and_remus/

40. https://www.researchhistory.org/2012/04/21/rome-founded/

41. https://www.britannica.com/biography/Romulus-and-Remus

42. https://scholarworks.umass.edu/server/api/core/bitstreams/fe814836-5e44-466e-a7d0-33c35fa02ca6/content

43. https://webplus.info/index.php?page=340&event=147204

44. https://carlos.emory.edu/htdocs/ODYSSEY/ROME/romulus.html

45. https://upload.wikimedia.org/wikipedia/commons/f/fb/Lupa_Capitolina,_Rome.jpg?sa=X&ved=2ahUKEwiHxrn0yLKMAxUgEkQIHSqMPPIQ_B16BAgBEAI

46. https://study.com/academy/lesson/romulus-and-remus-story-of-the-founding-of-rome.html

47. https://www.ebsco.com/research-starters/history/myth-romulus-and-remus

48. https://www.rome.net/romulus-and-remus

49. https://schoolhistory.co.uk/notes/romulus-and-remus/

50. https://en.wikipedia.org/wiki/Apis_(deity)

51. https://kids.britannica.com/students/article/Apis/309824

52. https://www.metmuseum.org/art/collection/search/552470

53. https://kids.britannica.com/students/article/Serapis/313409

54. https://www.magellantv.com/articles/by-the-horns-of-apis-ancient-egypts-noble-bullgod

55. https://leonmauldin.blog/2023/09/04/the-apis-bull-of-ancient-egypt/

56. https://www.wordforwordbiblecomic.com/blog/was-the-golden-calf-an-apis-bull

57. https://ancientegyptonline.co.uk/bullcult/

58. https://ancientegyptonline.co.uk/serapis/

59. https://egyptmythology.com/the-apis-bull-a-study-of-its-rituals-and-practices/

60. https://www.metmuseum.org/art/collection/search/570714

61. https://egyptatours.com/what-is-apis-bull/

62. https://en.wikipedia.org/wiki/Ptolemy_II_Philadelphus

63. https://www.worldhistory.org/Ptolemy_II_Philadelphus/

64. https://www.britannica.com/biography/Ptolemy-II-Philadelphus

65. https://nabataea.net/explore/history/ptolomy/

66. https://www.metmuseum.org/essays/egypt-in-the-ptolemaic-period

67. https://virtualreligion.net/iho/ptolemy_2.html

68. https://www.nytimes.com/2014/10/07/science/when-the-greeks-ruled-egypt-highlights-the-diversity-of-cultures-in-ptolemaic-egypt.html

69. https://sis.gov.eg/Story/1680/Alexander-the-Great-and-Ptolemy?lang=en-us

[1] https://en.wikipedia.org/wiki/Obelisk

[2]https://jurnal.umsu.ac.id/index.php/alhisab/article/download/21041/pdf_1

[3] https://www.centralparknyc.org/locations/obelisk

[4]https://www.instagram.com/ras_shaun2/reel/DGHdMKJO3Vr/

1. https://en.wikipedia.org/wiki/Hermes

2. https://en.wikipedia.org/wiki/Caduceus

3. https://sacred-texts.com/sym/mosy/mosy16.htm

4. https://www.newworldencyclopedia.org/entry/Caduceus

5. https://en.wikipedia.org/wiki/Mercury_(mythology)

6. https://blog.sciencemuseumgroup.org.uk/the-symbols-of-medicine/

7. http://drblayney.com/Asclepius.html

8. https://www.reddit.com/r/Kemetic/comments/11x4nkt/planets_of_the_gods/

9. https://en.wikipedia.org/wiki/Caduceus_as_a_symbol_of_medicine

Chapter 11

1. https://en.wikipedia.org/wiki/Ankh

2. https://en.wikipedia.org/wiki/Ancient_Egypt

3. https://study.com/learn/lesson/what-does-the-ankh-symbolize.html

4. https://www.worldhistory.org/Ankh/

5. https://allinonehighschool.com/nile-river-valley-civilization/

6. https://www.pyramidsland.com/blog/the-ankh-an-egyptian-symbol-for-life

7. https://eztouregypt.com/ankh-meaning/

8. https://visav.phys.uvic.ca/~babul/AstroCourses/P303/WebContent/egyptian.html

9. https://www.nps.gov/afbg/learn/historyculture/ankh.htm

https://www.luxorandaswan.com/blog/egyptian-history/egyptian-symbol-of-life

Chapter 12

[1]https://buyostrichfeathers.com/blogs/buy-ostrich-feathers-blog/cultural-significance-and-symbolism-of-ostrich-feathers

[2]http://www.enim-egyptologie.fr/revue/2012/1/EL-SAYED_ENIM5_p1-6.swf.pdf

[3] https://fancircleinternational.org/fans-of-tutankhamuns-tomb/

[4] http://tanveerbd.blogspot.com/2010/02/pharaohs-and-popes.html

[5]https://historicaleve.com/shuyet-ancient-egyptian-shadow/

[6]https://en.wikipedia.org/wiki/Fan-bearer_on_the_Right_Side_of_the_King

[7] https://www.thefanmuseum.org.uk/fan-history

[8] https://www.vaticannews.va/en/vatican-city/news/2021-05/vatican-egyptian-museum-mummies-ancient-egypt.html

[9]https://isac.uchicago.edu/sites/default/files/uploads/shared/docs/oimp35.pdf

[10]https://www.egypttoday.com/Article/4/120242/Meet-the-gilded-hand-fan-of-Tutankhamun

[11]https://www.historytoday.com/archive/natural-histories/tutankhamuns-ostriches

[12]https://www.instagram.com/miss_kentucky_05/p/C7kCtELPdzV/

[13]https://www.etsy.com/listing/1482122517/one-of-a-kind-king-tutankhamun-ostrich

[14]https://www.instagram.com/gems_in_gem/p/DGndDB0sVnd/

[15]https://www.egypttoursportal.com/blog/ancient-egyptian-civilization/ancient-egyptian-enemies/

[16]https://www.jacobusvandijk.nl/docs/Fs_van_Haarlem.pdf

[17] https://en.wikipedia.org/wiki/Battle_of_Kadesh

[18]http://web.ff.cuni.cz/ustavy/egyptologie/pdf/Gardiner_signlist.pdf

[19] https://www.youtube.com/watch?v=9wbI1VYraS0

[20]https://www.instagram.com/pyramidprintworks/p/CfCVLCuJO0y/

[21]https://www.reddit.com/r/Egypt/comments/hftub9/enemies_of_egypt/

[22]https://jarch.journals.ekb.eg/article_90999_77b5f811e8d22db458efb0b0dde3c990.pdf

[23] https://trove.nla.gov.au/newspaper/article/271992500

[24]https://www.academia.edu/60252216/The_Eighteenth_Dynasty_Titles_royal_nurse_mnt_nswt_royal_tutor_mn_nswt_and_foster_brother_sister_of_the_Lord_of_the_Two_Lands_sn_snt_mn_n_nb_t3wy_

[25]https://oi.uchicago.edu/sites/default/files/uploads/shared/docs/when_egypt.pdf

[26] https://en.wikipedia.org/wiki/Pope_Pius_XII

[27] https://www.touregypt.net/featurestories/fans.htm

[28]https://www.vaticannews.va/en/church/news/2023-10/what-the-vatican-and-pius-xii-knew-about-the-holocaust.html

[29]https://en.wikipedia.org/wiki/Papal_regalia_and_insignia

[30] https://en.wikipedia.org/wiki/Sandal-bearer

[31] https://www.pinterest.com/pin/72761350204877722/

[32]https://isac.uchicago.edu/sites/default/files/uploads/shared/docs/when_egypt.pdf

[33]https://www.nytimes.com/2010/03/08/nyregion/08pius.html

[34] https://egypt-museum.com/maiherpri/

[35]https://gillianlongworthmcguire.substack.com/p/egyptian-obelisks-in-rome

[36]https://newspapers.swco.ttu.edu/bitstream/handle/20.500.12255/266135/Big_Spring_Daily_Herald_1965_03_26.pdf?sequence=1&isAllowed=y

[37]https://sjam.journals.ekb.eg/article_302840_b2726a4acba5e4861d5a86fca6507ce4.pdf

[38] https://en.wikipedia.org/wiki/Mamdouh_Habib

[39]https://en.wikipedia.org/wiki/Ancient_Egyptian_royal_titulary

[40] https://austriaca.at/0xc1aa5576_0x00321da4.pdf

[41] https://time.com/archive/6659047/religion-door/

[42]https://www.almendron.com/tribuna/how-pope-francis-can-cleanse-the-far-right-rot-from-the-catholic-church/

[43]https://time.com/archive/6871154/religion-i-choose-john/